# The Secret of Childhood

MARIA MONTESSORI was born in Rome in 1870. She was the first woman medical graduate of the University of Rome. After working as Assistant Doctor in the clinic of Psychiatry, she was the Director (1898–1900) of the Scuola Ortofrenica, a school for children with special needs which had been founded as a result of her interest in such children. She also studied Philosophy at the University of Rome, with particular emphasis on the psychology of childhood, and lectured to students there in Pedagogical Anthropology. Around 1909, she developed the Montessori method, the famous system of education for children aged three to six, based on free discipline and free choice by children from stimulating learning apparatus provided to them. She was soon in charge of 50 schools for slum children called the Case dei Bambini in which her system was applied. From 1919 onwards she travelled round the world every other year conducting courses in teaching by the Montessori method, holding similar courses every alternate year in London. She died in 1952.

Her other books include *Pedagogical Anthropology*, *The Montessori Method*, *The Advanced Montessori Method* and *Montessori's Own Handbook*, most of which have been translated into several languages.

# The Secret of Childhood

## MARIA MONTESSORI

M.D. (Rome), D.Litt. (Durham), Ph.D. (Amsterdam)

*Translated and Edited by*
Barbara Barclay Carter
Lic-es-L. (Paris)

Orient BlackSwan

**ORIENT BLACKSWAN PRIVATE LIMITED**

*Registered Office*
3-6-752 Himayatnagar, Hyderabad 500 029 (A.P.), INDIA
e-mail: centraloffice@orientblackswan.com

*Other Offices*
Bangalore, Bhopal, Bhubaneshwar, Chandigarh, Chennai,
Ernakulam, Guwahati,Hyderabad, Jaipur, Kolkata,
Lucknow, Mumbai, New Delhi, Noida, Patna

ISBN: 978 81 250 3827 6

*Typeset in adobe Garamond 10.5/13 by*
*InoSoft Systems, Noida*

*Printed in India at*
Glorious Printers
Delhi

Published by
Orient Blackswan Private Limited
1/24 Asaf Ali Road, New Delhi 110 002
e-mail: delhi@orientblackswan.com

# Contents

*Foreword* by Krishna Kumar                                    ix

## I: THE SPIRITUAL EMBRYO

### 1. The Child To-day                                        **3**

The Century of the Child                                        3
The Child And Psycho-analysis                                   4
The Secret of Childhood                                         5
Accusation                                                      7

### 2. The Spiritual Embryo                                    **11**

Biological Prelude                                             11
The New-born Babe                                             14
Nature's Teaching                                             21
The Achievement of Incarnation                               23

### 3. Mind in the Making                                      **27**

The Sensitive Periods                                        27
The Care Required                                            34
Orientation Through Order                                    36
Inward Orientation                                          44
The Unfolding Intelligence                                  47

## 4. Where Adults Hinder 56

The Question of Sleep 56
Delight in Walking 60
Hand and Brain 63
Purposeful Activity 67

## 5. Rhythm 71

Rhythm 71
Adult Substitution 73
The Importance of Movement 77
"Intelligence of Love" 79

## II: THE NEW EDUCATION

## 6. The Task of the Educator 87

Discovery of the True Child 87
Spiritual Preparation 89

## 7. Our Own Method 95

How it Originated 95
"Who are You?" 97
The First Children 100
What They Showed Me 102

## 8. Further Developments 118

The Principles Established 118
Messina Orphans 121
Well-to-do Children 124
True Normality 128

## 9. Psychic Deviations 130

Their Single Cause 130
Fugues 131
"Barriers" 133

The Dependent Child 137
Possessiveness 138
The Power Craving 140
The Inferiority Complex 142
Fear 145
Lying 147
Repercussions on Physical Life 150

## III: THE CHILD AND SOCIETY

### 10. Homo Laborans 157

The Conflict Between Child and Adult 157
The Instinct to Work 158
The Characteristics of the Two Kinds of Work 160
The Adult's Task 161
The Child's Task 163
The Two Tasks Compared 165
Growth Through Activity 167
Guiding Instincts 170

### 11. The Child as Master 178

"Know Thyself" 178
The Parents' Mission 180
The Rights of the Child 181
Ecce Homo 188

# Foreword

*Krishna Kumar*

The world has now entered an altogether new cycle of conflicts. Sources of hope for peace, cultivated during the latter half of the twentieth century, arouse little confidence. People who work with children notice in them a remarkably early growth of cynicism towards aspirations other than the purely .personal and material. The idea that children represent a new world or a future which will be different from the present seems unconvincing. It is hardly surprising that in such an ethos, the desperate demand for values in education, or rather values *through* education, is getting louder. Such a demand reflects the general despair but cannot address it.

This is an appropriate moment for the rediscovery of Montessori, or rather of her deeper message, for the method she invented has enjoyed popularity, at least of a superficial kind, all along. *The Secret of Childhood* was first published in 1936 when a second terrible war had already acquired a certain amount of inevitability. In the world of education, methods derived from the ideology of behaviourism were dominant and the scholarly challenge this ideology was to face from cognitive psychology had not manifested. Montessori's discovery of the child's 'secret' offered, at such a time, both an immediate relief and a longer vision and hope for change in education. This was also the time when in the context of the war, her incarceration in India created a fortuitous situation for a deeper personal bond to form between her and India.

All key concepts which form the edifice of Montessori's thought are available in this book, and hence it can easily serve as an invitation. But an invitation to what? If we answer this question by merely referring to the pedagogic techniques and advice Montessori offered, we will miss the vital part of her contribution and legacy. The adventure this book invites us to join in is the world of knowledge about childhood. It enables us to get a glimpse of the psychic life that the newborn child's mind is in touch with, but which it shortly loses when it is forced into a conflict with adults and their world. Montessori's description of this conflict is quite unique in the history of educational thought. Her description is also quite brutal as it reminds us of the depths to which our unimaginative ways of dealing with children in the name of education can descend.

The promise of a peaceful world that Montessori held out and worked for, rests on the condition that we let each child reveal her or his self, in the course of development. Such a natural thing has become virtually impossible today, so tough are our regime and demands. Montessori's plea is for creating an environment marked by aesthetic care and awareness, and for a style of teaching which interferes as little as possible with the child's own pursuits. Quite often one finds that her pedagogic advice is heard, and even applied, without adequate appreciation of the larger theory. *The Secret of Childhood* is an important book because it enables us to grasp Montessori's theory and thereby to desist from applying her advice mechanically.

# PART I

# The Spiritual Embryo

# 1

# The Child Today

## THE CENTURY OF THE CHILD

The amazingly rapid progress in the care and education of children in recent years may be attributed partly to a generally higher standard of life, but still more to an awakening of conscience. Not only is there an increasing concern for child health—it began in the last decade of the 19th century—but also a new awareness of the personality of the child as something of the highest importance. To-day it is impossible to go deeply into any branch of medicine or philosophy or sociology without taking account of the contribution brought by a knowledge of child life. A parallel, but on a lesser scale, is the light thrown by embryology on physiology in general and on evolution. But the study of the child, not in his physical but in his psychological aspect, may have an infinitely wider influence, extending to all human questions. In the mind of the child we may perhaps find the key to progress and who knows, the beginning of a new civilisation.

The Swedish poet and author Ellen Key prophesied that our century would be the century of the child. While anyone with patience to hunt through historical documents would find a recurrence of such ideas in the first King's Speech of King Victor Emmanuel III of Italy, when in 1900, at the turn of the century, he succeeded to the throne after the assassination of his predecessor. He spoke of the new era beginning with the new century, and he too spoke of it as the Century of the Child.

It would, seem that such almost prophetic glimpses arose from the impression produced by the investigations of science in the last ten years of the 19th century; from the picture they gave of the child in sickness, ten times more exposed than the adult to death from infectious disease, or of the child as victim in harsh schools. No one could have foreseen then that the child held within himself a secret of life, able to lift the veil from the mysteries of the human soul; that he represented an unknown quantity, the discovery of which might enable the adult to solve his individual and social problems. This aspect may prove the foundation of a new science of child study, capable of influencing the whole social life of man.

## THE CHILD AND PSYCHO-ANALYSIS

Psycho-analysis has thrown open a realm of research formerly unknown, bringing to light the secrets of the unconscious, but it has brought no practical solution to the urgent practical problems of life. None the less, it may help us to understand the contribution to be found in the hidden life of the child.

Psycho-analysis has, one might say, broken through the cortex of consciousness, which psychology had previously considered as a *ne plus ultra*, like the Columns of Hercules in ancient history, which for the Greek seamen, were limits beyond which superstition set the edge of the world.

Psycho-analysis has sounded the ocean of the unconscious. Without this discovery it would be hard to explain to the public at large how the child mind may help in a more searching study of human problems. As is well known, psycho-analysis began as a new technique for the cure of mental diseases and was hence a branch of medicine. It made a truly illuminating discovery in establishing the power of the unconscious over human actions. It has been, as it were, a tudy of psychic reactions behind consciousness, of responses which bring to light hidden factors and unsuspected realities, revolutionising accepted ideas. They reveal the existence of an unknown world of vast extent, with which, one might say, the destiny of the individual is bound up. But psycho-analysis cannot fully explore this unknown world. In Charcot's time, in the last century, psychiatry discovered the subconscious. Just as in a volcano the seething elements in the core of the earth force their way to the surface, the subconscious was seen to manifest itself in exceptional cases in the graver states of mental disease. Hence its strange phenomena, conflicting with the manifestations of consciousness, were considered merely as symptoms of disease. Freud took a contrary path. By a laborious technique he found the way to penetrate to the unconscious, but till recently he too tended to confine himself to the domain of pathology. For how many normal persons would willingly submit to the painful tests of psycho-analysis? To a kind of operation on the soul? It was thus from his treatment of the sick that Freud deduced his psychological theories, and the new psychology was in large measure built up on personal deductions drawn from abnormality. Hence Freud's theories have proved inadequate, nor has his technique of treating the sick been wholly satisfactory, for it has not always led to a healing of "sickness of the soul". As a result, social traditions, which are the deposit of ancient experience, have risen as a barrier against certain generalisations of Freudian theory. Perhaps, the exploration of the vast reality of the unconscious requires something quite other than a technique of clinical treatment or theoretical deductions.

## THE SECRET OF CHILDHOOD

The task of sounding this ocean of the unconscious remains for other branches of science and demands another approach—the study of man from his origins, in an endeavour to decipher in the child soul its development through conflict with its environment, to learn the dramatic or tragic secret of the struggles through which the soul of man has remained disfigured and darkened.

Psycho-analysis touched this secret. One of the most impressive discoveries due to its technique was how a psychosis may originate in the distant age of infancy. The memories evoked from the subconscious proved that in infancy there were sufferings other than those commonly known and which lay so latent in consciousness, so far from accepted ideas, that their discovery was the most impressive and perturbing of all the discoveries of psycho-analysis. Such sufferings were of a purely psychic order, slow and constant; they had never been recognised as facts liable to lead to psychic sickness of the adult personality. They sprang from the *repression* of the spontaneous activity of the child by the adult who had authority over him, and were therefore to be associated with the adult whose influence was greatest—the mother.

We must draw a clear distinction between the two planes of enquiry covered by psycho-analysis. One, the more superficial, covers the clash between the instincts of the individual and the environment to which he must adapt himself. This conflict may be resolved; for it is not difficult to bring to consciousness the disturbing causes that lie below consciousness. But there is also another, deeper plane, that of infant memories in which the conflict is not between man and his present social environment, but between the child and the mother, or, we may say generally, between the child and the adult. This conflict may lead to disea᷼ far harder to cure. In all diseases, physical as well as mental, the importance of events that have occurred in infancy is now recognised. But here some other method than psycho-analysis is needed. The very technique of sounding the unconscious that allows discoveries to be made in the case of adults, becomes an obstacle in the case of the child. The child, who by nature is not a fit subject for such technique, has not to remember his infancy. He lives his childhood. He must be observed rather than analysed, but observed from the psychic standpoint in an endeavour to ascertain the conflict through which he passes in his relations with grown-up persons and with his social environment. It is clear that this approach will lead us away from psycho-analytic theories and technique into a new field of observation of the child in his social existence. It is not a case of the tortuous labyrinths of a sick mind, but of the wide expanse of human life in its reality, centering round the psychological life of the child; for the practical problem embraces the whole life of man as it develops from birth onwards.

The page of human history that tells the adventures of man as mind has yet to be read—of the child whose sensitivity encounters obstacles and who finds himself involved in insuperable conflicts with the grown-up who is stronger than he, who masters him without understanding him. Here was a blank page that had yet to receive the story of the unrealised sufferings that convulse the intact and delicate spiritual existence of the child, organising in his subconscious a lower man, different from what nature had intended.

This complex question psycho-analysis illuminates, but does not solve. Psycho-analysis deals mainly with disease and remedial treatment. The problem of the child psyche contains a prophylactic where psycho-analysis is concerned; for it will affect the normal and general treatment of infant humanity, a treatment that helps to avert obstacles and conflicts and hence their consequences—the psychological diseases dealt with by psycho-analysis, or else those moral maladjustments which extend to nearly the whole of humanity.

Round the child, therefore, a new field of scientific exploration has come into being, distinct from psycho-analysis, its sole parallel. It implies essentially a form of assistance to the psychic life of infancy, and is concerned with normality and with education. Its characteristic is therefore the ascertainment of psychological facts as yet unknown with regard to the child, and at the same time an awakening of the adult, who, in regard to the child, adopts mistaken attitudes that have their root in the subconscious.

## ACCUSATION

The word *repression* as used by Freud to indicate the deep-seated origins of psychological disturbances in the adult explains itself.

The child cannot expand in the manner required by a being in process of development, for the adult represses him. "The adult" is an abstraction. The child is isolated in society, so if the adult influences him, that adult is a given adult, the adult closest to him—his mother first, then his father, then his teachers.

Society attributes to adults quite another role, giving them the credit of the education and development of the child. Now, on the contrary, the sounding of the depths of the soul brings to light an *accusation* against those who have been recognised as the guardians and benefactors of humanity. But since almost all are fathers or mothers and many are teachers or entrusted with the care of children, the accusation covers the adult world in general, the society responsible for the children. This startling accusation has something apocalyptic about it; it is mysterious and terrible like the voice of the Last Judgment: "What have you done with the children that I entrusted to you?"

The first reaction is one of self-defence, of protest: "We did our best. We love our children. We sacrificed ourselves for them." And this juxtaposes two conflicting attitudes, the one conscious, the other rising from what is unconscious. The defence is familiar, it is old and deep-rooted and holds no interest for us. What is of interest is the accusation, or rather those whom it envisages. They struggle and strive to perfect the care and education of their children, and they find themselves caught in a network of problems, for they do not know the error they harbour in themselves.

All who preach in favour of the child must maintain this accusation against the adult, an accusation without remission, without exception. And all at once, this accusation becomes a centre of fascinating interest; for it denounces not merely *involuntary* errors, but errors of which we are wholly *unconscious,* and therefore it increases our stature, leading us to the discovery of ourselves. And every true advance comes from the discovery, the utilisation of the unknown.

For this reason, in every age the attitude of men towards their own errors has been contradictory. Everyone is offended by conscious error, and is attracted and fascinated by unknown error. Unknown error holds the secret of progress beyond the goal that is known and desired, and raises us to a higher realm. Thus the mediaeval knight who was ready to fight a duel at the smallest accusation that impinged on his conscious code would prostrate himself before the altar, saying humbly, "I am guilty, I declare it before all and the fault is mine alone." The Bible gives interesting examples of such contradictions. What was it that brought the crowd round Jonah at Nineveh, so that King and people were filled with enthusiasm, and thronged the streets in the wake of the prophet? He proclaimed them such appalling sinners that if they were not converted Nineveh would be destroyed. How did John the Baptist summon the crowds to the bank of the Jordan, what alluring terms did he employ to obtain such an extraordinary concourse of people? He called them a "brood of vipers."

Here is a spiritual phenomenon—men who flock to hear themselves accused. And by so doing they assent, they admit their fault. There are harsh and insistent charges that summon the unconscious to consciousness; all spiritual development is an achievement of consciousness, which assumes into itself what was once outside it. It is thus, indeed, that civilisation advances, by successive discoveries.

Now, if the child is to receive a different treatment from what it receives to-day, in order to save it from conflicts endangering its psychic life, there is a first, fundamental, essential step to be taken, from which all will depend—the modification of the adult. Indeed if the adult is already doing all he can, and, as he will say, loves the child to the point of sacrifice, he acknowledges that he is faced by an insuperable problem. He must necessarily seek beyond what is known, voluntary and conscious.

Even in the child there is much that is unknown. There is a part of the soul of the child that has always been unknown, and that must be known. In the child, too, there is need for the discovery that will lead us to the unknown; for besides the child observed and studied by psychology and education, there remains the unknown child. We must seek for him in a spirit of enthusiasm, like those who know of hidden gold, and who explore unknown lands and move mountains in search of the precious metal. This is what the adult must do in searching for this unknown something hidden in the soul of the child. This is the labour in which all must partake, without distinction of caste, race or nation; for it will mean the bringing forth of an indispensable factor for the moral progress of humanity.

The adult has not understood the child or the adolescent and is therefore in continual strife with him. The remedy is not that the adult should learn something intellectually, or complete a deficient culture. He must find a different starting-point. The adult must find in himself the hitherto unknown error that prevents him from seeing the child as he is. If this preparation is wanting, and if he has not acquired the aptitude that such preparation entails, he cannot proceed further. The act of self-knowledge is not as difficult as is supposed, for all error, even though unconscious, means suffering and anguish, and a single hint at the remedy brings perception of acute need. Thus a man who has a finger out of joint feels the need to have it put in place, for he realises that his hand cannot work or his pain cease till this is done. In the same way, as soon as he understands his error, man feels the need to set his conscience in order; for from that moment the weakness and pain that he has long borne become intolerable. And once this has been done, all becomes easy. No sooner do we come to the conviction that we had taken too much credit to ourselves, that we had believed ourselves able to do what lay beyond our sphere and our possibilities, than it becomes possible and interesting to recognise the characteristics of souls as diverse from our own as those of children.

The adult has become egocentric in relation to the child, not egotistic, but egocentric. Thus he considers everything that affects the psyche of the child from the standpoint of its reference to himself, and so misunderstands the child. It is this point of view that leads to a consideration of the child as an empty being, which the adult must fill by his own endeavours, as an *inert and incapable being* for whom everything must be done, as a being without an *inner guide,* whom the adult must guide step by step from without. Finally, the adult acts as though he were the child's creator, and considers good and evil in the child's actions from the standpoint of its relation to himself. The adult is the touchstone of good and evil. He is infallible; he is the good on which the child must model himself. Any way in which the child departs from the characteristics of the adult is an evil that must be speedily corrected. And in adopting such an attitudes, which unconsciously *cancels the child's personality*, the adult feels a connection of zeal, love and sacrifice.

# 2

# The Spiritual Embryo

## BIOLOGICAL PRELUDE

When Wolff announced his discoveries on the segmentation of the germ-cell, he threw new light on the process of the creation of living creatures, and at the same time made it possible to verify, by direct observation, the existence of inner forces working in accordance with a pre-determined pattern. It was he who overthrew certain philosophical ideas, like those of Leibniz and Spallanzani, by which the germ was supposed to contain in miniature the complete form of the future creature. They supposed that in the ovum, that is to say from the beginning, the being that would develop if brought into a favourable environment was already formed, albeit imperfectly and in infinitesimal proportions. This idea came from the observation of the seed of a plant, which contains, hidden between the two cotyledons, a tiny plant in which we can recognise root and leaves and which, set in the earth, develops into the new plant. It was supposed that an analogous process held good for animals and for man.

But when Wolff, after the discovery of the microscope, was able to observe how a living being is really formed (he began by observing the embryos of birds), he found that the first stage is a simple germ-cell, in which the microscope, by its very power to render visible what is invisible to the naked eyeshows that there is no pre-existent form at all. The germ-cell, which results from the union of two cells, male and female, consists simply of membrane, protoplasm and nucleus like every other cell; indeed, it is merely a simple cell, in its most primary form, without any visible differentiation. Every living creature, whether plant or animal, comes from a primary, simple and undifferentiated cell. The tiny plant within the seed is an embryo that has already developed from the germ-cell; it completed its earlier stages in the fruit, from which the ripened seed fell to earth.

The germ-cell, however, possesses a most singular property, that of rapid subdivision, and of subdivision on a pre-established pattern. But of this pattern there is not the smallest trace in the original cell. If we follow the earliest developments of the animal embryo, we see the first cell split into two, these two into four, and so on, till they form a kind of hollow ball, known as the morula, which next introflects into two layers, leaving an aperture, and forming a kind of hollow double-walled cavity, the gastrula. And thus by continued multiplication, introflexion and differentiation, it develops into a complicated whole of organs and tissues. The germ-cell, therefore, simple, transparent and devoid of any material design, works and builds in exact obedience to the immaterial order it bears within itself—like a faithful servant who knows by heart the mission he has received and who fulfils it, though carrying on his person no document that could reveal the secret order he has been given. The design is discernible only through the activity of the indefatigable cells, and we can see only the completed work. Beyond the completed work nothing exists.

In the embryos of mammals, and hence of men, the first organ to appear is the heart, or rather, that which will become the heart—a vesicle that begins at once to beat in a regular rhythm, beating twice for each beat of the heart of the mother. And it will continue to beat unwearying; for it is the vital motor that enables all the vital tissues to form, pulsing to them the nourishment they need for life.

All this labour is hidden, and is wonderful precisely because it is done thus alone. It is the miracle of creation from almost nothing. Those wise little living cells never make mistakes, and find in themselves the power for far-reaching transformations, some becoming cartilage cells, some nerve cells, some skin cells, and each tissue finds its exact place. This marvel of creation is one of the secrets of the universe, rigorously kept; nature envelops it in impenetrable veils and sheaths, and she alone can part them, when finally, matured and complete, a new creature is born into the world.

But the creature that is born is not merely a material body. It, in its turn, is like a germ-cell, possessing latent psychic functions, of predetermined type. The new body does not function through its organs only; it has other functions—the urges which cannot be seated in a cell but in a living body, in a creature already born. Just as every germ-cell bears within itself the pattern of the organism-to-be, though without visible sign, so every new-born body, whatever its species, bears in itself a pattern of psychical instinct, of functions that will set it in relation to its environment, for the fulfilment of a cosmic mission. And this whatever the creature, even in an insect. The marvellous instincts of bees, which lead them to so complex a social organisation, begin to work only in the bee, not in the egg or in the grub. The instinct of flight is in the bird after it is born, and not before. And so on. This second phase which concerns psychic life in relation to the outer environment is inherent in the first, in the embryonic life that nature isolates and hides. Indeed when the new creature is formed it is like a spiritual egg, bearing within it a mysterious guidance, which will result in acts, characters, labours, in short, in functions acting upon its outer environment.

This outer environment must provide not only the means of physiological existence, but stimuli to the mysterious mission inscribed in every creature that is born, all of which are summoned by their environment not only to life but to the exercise of a necessary office for the conservation of the world and its harmony. Each according to its species. The body has precisely the shape adapted to this psychic superfunction, which must take its place in the economy of the universe. That such higher functions are inherent in creatures as soon as they are born we see from the animals. We know that one mammal will be peaceable, because it is a lamb, that another will be fierce because it is a lion, that one insect will labour without ceasing in unchanging discipline because it is an ant, and that another will do nothing but chirp in solitude because it is a cricket.

And thus the new-born child is not only a body ready to function as a body, but a spiritual embryo with latent psychic capacities. It would be absurd to think that man alone, characterised and distinct from all other creatures by the grandeur of his mental life, should be the only one with no pattern of psychic development.

The spirit may be so profoundly latent that it will not be apparent like the instinct of the animal, which is at once ready to reveal itself in given actions. The absence of fixed and determined guiding instincts, such as are possessed by the animals, is the sign of a fund of freedom of action, demanding a special elaboration, almost as though it had to be created and developed by each individual, and were therefore unpredictable. There is thus a secret in the soul of the child, impossible to penetrate unless he himself reveals it as little by little he builds up his being. It is the same as in the segmentation of the germ-cell, where there is nothing but an invisible pre-determined pattern, which there is no means of discerning and which will manifest itself only with the gradual creation of the details of the organism. And therefore only the child can bring revelation of the *natural pattern of man*. But because of the delicacy of all creation from nothing, the psychic life of the child needs a defence and an environment analogous to the sheaths and veils that nature has set round the physical embryo.

### THE NEW-BORN BABE

"A quivering voice was heard on the earth.

It had never been heard before.

It came from a throat that had never stirred before.

"They told me of a man who had lived in the deepest darkness: his eyes had never seen the faintest glimmer, as though he were in the depth of an abyss.

"They told me of a man who had lived in silence, not even the faintest sound had ever reached his ears....

"I heard tell of a man who had really lived, always under water, a water of strange warmth, and who all at once was plunged into an icy stream.

"And he unfolded lungs that had never breathed. The air all at once distended his lungs, which had been folded from the beginning and the man cried out....

"And a quivering voice was heard on the earth. It had never been heard before. It came from a throat that had never stirred before.

"He was the man who had rested.

"Who can imagine such absolute rest?

"The rest of one who has not had even the trouble of eating, for another ate for him. All his fibres were relaxed, for other tissues created the heat necessary to his life. Even his inmost tissues had not to work to defend themselves from poisons and microbes, for other tissues worked for him. And oxygen was given him without his breathing—a privilege unique among living creatures.

"His only labour was that of the heart, which beat before he existed. Yes, even when he did not yet exist, his heart was beating at twice the rate of any other heart. It was the heart of a man.

"And now.... He comes forward. He takes upon himself all labour. He is wounded by light and by sound, travailed in the inmost fibres of his being, and as he advances he gives the great cry:

"Why hast Thou forsaken me?

"And thus, for the first time, man reflects in himself the Christ who dies and the Christ who ascends."

\* \* \*

The new-born child does not come into a natural environment, but into the civilised environment of the life of men. It is a "supranatural" environment, built up above and at the expense of nature, through the urge to procure all that will assist the life of man in all its details and make it easier for him to adjust himself. But what providence has prepared a civilisation to assist the new-born babe, man who must achieve the greatest of all efforts at adjustment, when he passes by birth from one life to another?

The tremendous transition of birth demands a scientific treatment of the new-born babe, for in no other period of man's life will he find a like occasion of struggle and conflict, and hence of suffering.

But no provision is made to ease this tremendous passage. In the history of human civilisation a page should be set before all others, telling what civilised man does to help the newly born. But here, indeed, the paper is blank.

Many will say that, on the contrary, civilisation takes a great deal of thought for the new-born child.

How does it do so?

When a child is born, all concern goes to the mother. The mother has suffered so greatly.

But has not the child suffered too?

The mother needs special care.

But does not the child, too, need special care?

The mother's room is darkened and silent, for she is worn out.

But it is the child who has just come from a place where not the faintest ray of light, or the faintest sound, could reach him. It is for him, then, that darkness and silence should be prepared.

The child has come from absolute rest, and has now, all at once, to exercise all his functions.

He, therefore, must be tired and exhausted.

His exhaustion does not come only from the contrast between two opposite environments; he has just endured the exhausting labour of birth by his own efforts. His body was compressed, as though in a mill, that squeezed it to the point of displacing its bones. He arrives worn out by the immense contrast between absolute rest and the inconceivable effort of birth.

He is like a pilgrim who comes from somewhere far distant, worn out and wounded. And what do we do to receive him, to succour him in so great a need?

The doctor casts only a superficial glance at the new-born babe, to see if it is alive. He probably thinks, "It is alive, so put it on one side, we cannot bother with it now."

The parents, on the contrary, gaze on it with tenderness and joy, and they welcome it with the egotism of those who rejoice in a gift from nature: "The fine baby? Our son?"

All those who awaited him are impatient to enjoy him, to admire him, to touch him. The father will want to see the colour of his eyes, and will try to open the eyelids of the new creature, gazing eagerly, and smiling for joy as he sees the pupils that will one day see him and recognise him.

But no one sees in the new-born babe the suffering man, the first image of Christ, pure and incomprehended.

How does the adult approach the being who comes from nothing, and who finds himself in the world with those delicate eyes that have never seen light, those ears that have been engulfed in silence? This creature with tortured limbs that have till then touched nothing?

The delicate body is exposed to brutal contact with solid objects, it is handled by the soulless hands of a grown-up man, who forgets its delicacy.

Yes, the new-born babe is roughly handled, its delicate skin is rubbed by heavy hands, by rough cloths.

Indeed, the family hardly dare touch it, so fragile is it; its relations and its mother look on it with fear, and so they entrust it to *expert hands,* and set their minds at rest; conscience has found a refuge where it can be at ease. No one will feel the need to watch over and defend that little body that had known no touch before.

People will ask, "What then should we do? Someone must touch the baby."

Yes, but those expert hands that now touch it have never learned how to touch such a delicate creature. They are rough hands, with the sole ability to hold the baby securely, without letting it fall. People think that if the baby, having passed through birth, is alive, that is enough; all they seek is that the effort of existence should not be lost. But they have never studied how to approach this delicate being.

The doctor picks it up roughly, and as the new-born baby gives its despairing cry, all smile in satisfaction: that is its voice. Weeping is its language, and such things are necessary for it, to wash its eyes and distend its lungs.

The new-born child is immediately clothed.

Once it was wrapped in rigid swaddling clothes, as if it were set in plaster, and its limbs, which from the beginning had been folded together, were stretched out and fixed with cruel force.

Yet it is not necessary to clothe the baby, neither immediately after nor during the first month of life.

If we want to follow the story of the clothing of new-born babies, we find a gradual evolution, from rigid supports to soft, light clothing, with a gradual decrease in the size of its wardrobe. To-day, indeed, the clothing of the newly born is on the threshold of nudism. One step more, and it will be left naked.

Indeed, it should be best if the baby could be left naked, to be kept warm by the surrounding air and not by clothes. It has not sufficient heat in itself to face the temperature outside, since it has lived till now in the warmth of the maternal body. Clothes can only preserve the heat of the body, preventing it from escaping. If the room is warmed, clothes become an obstacle between the warmth of the air and the child's body. We notice among the animals that even when the little ones are covered with fur or fluff, the mother covers them with her body to keep them warm.

We do not want to dwell too long on this argument. Assuredly, if they were able to speak to me, Americans would tell me of the care that is taken of new-born children in their country, and Germans and English would ask me in surprise, if I am unaware of the progress made in their countries in this branch of medicine and nursing. And still, I should have to answer that I know all this, and that I have gone in person to study all the latest refinements in childcare in certain of these countries. And all the same, I have to declare that everywhere there is a lack of that nobility of conscience demanded for a worthy welcome to the man that is born.

It is true that much is done, but what is progress if it is not an awareness of that of which we were once aware, and adding to what seemed complete, and even unsurpassable?

Nowhere in the world is the baby understood as it should be.

I should like to touch on another point—the fact that however deeply we love the new baby, we have an instinct of defence against him, from the first instant of his arrival. It is not only an instinct of defence, but an instinct of avarice, that makes us hasten to protect our possessions from him however worthless they be in themselves. For example, to save his wretched little mattress from being soiled, we set a waterproof covering between it and his body, and allow his body to suffer the consequences.

From that moment, the adult mind will move to the same rhythm: take care that the baby shall not soil me, not be a nuisance. Defence against him!

\* \* \*

I believe that as little by little humanity acquires a fuller understanding of the child, it will find greatly improved methods of care. Only very recently has a beginning been made, in Vienna, of ways of lessening the sufferings of the new-born baby. The bit of mattress on which it must fall in birth is warmed, and mattresses have been invented of absorbent material, that can be thrown away as soon as they are soiled. These expedients are a prelude, a first sign of a fact of immense importance—that the consciousness of the adult is beginning to be aware of the baby.

But the care of the new-born baby should not be limited to preserving it from death, to isolating it from infection, as is done today in the more modern clinics where the nurses who approach it cover their faces with bandages so that the microbes from their breath shall not reach it. There are the problems of the "psychic care of the child", from the very moment of birth—and those of measures to facilitate his adjustment to the world. To this end, experiments have still to be made in clinics, and propaganda is required in families in order that the attitude towards the newly born should be changed.

In rich families people still think of grand cradles and fine lace for the baby's clothing. Such luxury shows a complete absence of consideration for the child's inner being. Wealth should be employed in provision of comfort, not of luxury, for such privileged children.

For the baby it would be a comfort to have a room sheltered from the noise of the town, with sufficient silence, and a light that can be moderated and corrected as, for example, is done in churches by stained glass windows. A warm, constant temperature, such as has for some years been obtainable in operating theatres, should allow the child to lie naked.

Another problem is that of moving and carrying the naked child, so that it should be touched as little as possible by the hands. The child should be picked up by means of a light, yielding support, like a softly stuffed hammock, supporting the whole body gathered together in a position resembling that of pre-natal conditions. Such supporters should be handled with great delicacy and deliberation, by clean hands rendered skilful by careful practice. To change the position of the child from vertical to horizontal calls for special skill. Nurses have for long realised that a special technique is required for lifting a sick person and carrying him horizontally and slowly. The transport of the sick is one of the elementary lessons of nursing. No one pulls a sick person up vertically by the arm: he is moved by means of a yielding support, delicately introduced under his body, and by this method he can be moved without changing his horizontal position.

Now the new-born baby is like a sick person. Like its mother, it has passed through peril of death. The joy and satisfaction of seeing it alive is also relief at the danger it has escaped. Sometimes the baby is almost suffocated, and has to be brought to life by the rapid administration of an artificial respiration. Its head is often deformed by a haematoma, that is, by a flow of blood beneath the skin. It must then be considered really sick. But at the same time the new-born baby must not be confused with a sick adult. Its needs are not those of a sick person, but of one who makes an inconceivable effort of readjustment, accompanied by the first mental impressions of a being that has come from nothing, but whose senses are active. I have seen a new-born baby that had been barely saved from a dangerous condition of suffocation, plunged into a basin almost on the level of the ground, and, as it was rapidly lowered into the water, it opened its eyes wide and gave a convulsive leap, stretching out its arms and legs, as though it felt itself falling. That was its first experience of fear.

The feeling we should have towards the new-born baby is not the compassion that we have for the sick or weak, but reverence before the mystery of creation, the secret of an infinite taking bounded form.

The manner of handling the new-born babe and the delicacy of feeling that should inspire such handling make one think of the Catholic priest as he handles the Host at the altar. With purified hands, which have practised every detail of their movement, with what delicacy and deliberation does he move the Host, now vertically, now horizontally, setting It down from time to time, as if It were weary, as if even such movements were so vigorous as to need interruption. And while he raises up the Host, he prostrates himself in worship. There is silence; the light that enters is subdued by coloured glass; a feeling of hope, of elevation, fills the whole environment; such is the environment worthy of the child.

* * *

The baby, people say, is not conscious, and without consciousness there can be neither pain nor pleasure, such refinements would therefore be wasted on it. But how much care is lavished on sick adults whose life is in danger and who are unconscious? It is the need of care and not the consciousness of that need that, in respect of every other age of human life, calls for the attention of science and feeling.

No justification is possible.

We have no real feeling for the new-born baby; for us it is not human. When it comes into our world, we do not know how to receive it, although the world that we have created is destined for it, so that it may continue it and make of it a better world than ours.

"He came into the world, and the world was made by him but the world knew him not. He came unto his own and his own received him not."

## NATURE'S TEACHING

The higher animals, the mammals, in the unchanging wisdom of instinct, have not overlooked the delicate and difficult period of adjustment that faces their new-born young. The humble cat is an example; she *hides* her kittens as soon as they are born, finding some dark, remote place in which to keep them, and she is so jealous that she does not allow people even to look at them. And then, after a short period, they come out and follow her openly.

Mammals in a free state give still more striking proofs of their care for the new-born. The greater number live together in numerous herds, but the female near delivery leaves the herd and finds a hidden place where she gives birth to her young, keeping them in silence and isolation for a period of time that varies according to the species from two or three weeks to a month or more. The mother becomes immediately a nurse helping the new creature. The little one could not exist among the herd, exposed to light and noise, and therefore she keeps it in a quiet, sheltered place. Although the young one can generally stand on its legs and walk, the mother keeps it apart till it has attained mastery over its vital functions and has adapted itself to the new environment. After that she leads it back to the herd, to the society of its kind.

The tale of such maternal care is really remarkable; it is substantially uniform, even among species as different as horses, bisons, boars, foxes and tigers.

The cow-bison stays away from the herd many weeks, alone with her calf, tending it with great affection. When it is cold she holds it between her front hooves, when it is dirty, she licks it clean; when it is sucking she stands on three legs so that it may get at the milk more easily. Later she leads it back to her own herd, and continues to suckle it with the patient indifference we find among female quadrupeds.

Sometimes the mother does not only seek isolation for her delivery, but works to prepare an appropriate place for the expected young. The vixen, for instance, seeks in a thick covert for a remote, quiet place, such as a cave, that may serve for dwelling. If she finds no suitable place, she digs a hole, or she prepares a bed in a hollow tree, or hollows out a thick bush; then she makes a nest, lined with soft material and almost always with her own fur, which she tears out round her dugs, thus making it easier for the cubs to suck. And there her six or seven cubs are born, with closed eyes and ears; she keeps them hidden and hardly ever leaves them.

All mother beasts during this period guard their young jealously, and attack anyone who approaches them. Such instincts are overlaid or lost when the animals live in a domestic state. It is a well-known fact that sows often eat their young, whereas the female of the wild boar is one of the tenderest mothers. Tigresses and lionesses also, in a state of captivity, in cages or in zoological gardens, sometimes kill their children. We thus see that nature's protective and providential energies only function when creatures are free to follow the inner commands of their guiding instincts.

In such instincts we may trace a clear and simple logic; the new-born young of mammals must be cared for in a special manner during the *first encounter with the outer world;* and there is, therefore, need to distinguish a first, extremely delicate period, that of the creature's first advent into the world, when it must rest after the immense effort of birth and assume the simultaneous mastery of all its functions. After this period begins what we may call first infancy, the first year of life, the sucking period, that is to say, the first period of life in the world.

The animals by isolating their new-born young do not care only for their bodies. Nature indeed, by milk and the warmth of the maternal body, has already provided against the main physical difficulties to be overcome in the new environment. The mother rather waits in this solitude for the psychical awakening of instincts that spring from the inmost being of the new creature and will make it another individual of its race. This awakening must come about in a place sheltered from bright light or loud noises and in an unbroken quiet. It is for this that the mother waits, as she feeds, cleans and lovingly helps her offspring, and to this end she trains it before leading it back to the herd. The colt by that time will be lively on its legs, it will have learned to know its mother and to follow her, but above all it will have had time for the *horse nature* to reveal itself in its frail and hesitant body. It must bring its heredity to realisation. The mare will not allow her offspring to be seen by any till it has become truly a little horse; the cat will hide her kittens till their eyes have opened, and they have learned to stand on their feet, till, in short, they are truly little cats.

It is plain that nature exercises a powerful supervision over this awakening, this fulfilment. The aim of the mother's care is higher than purely physiological. Through her affection and her tender care, she awaits the birth of the latent instincts. And for men we might say by analogy that, through delicate care of the new-born babe, we should await the spiritual advent of the man.

## THE ACHIEVEMENT OF INCARNATION

Is there then a *psychic life* to be considered in the treatment of the new-born child? If it exists already in the new-born child, it must be considered still more during the first year of life and later. The forward step that has been made in the care of the child to-day is this: that account is taken not only of his physical life, but of his psychic life. It is now often repeated that education should begin from birth.

Of course, the word 'education' must not be understood in the sense of teaching, but of assisting the psychological development of the child. Now that a distinction is drawn between consciousness and the unconscious it is possible to understand how the baby may have a real psychic life from the moment it is born. The idea of an unconscious full of psychic impulses and realities has become one of the popular arguments of our age. If we envisage the baby with a psychic life, with the need to develop its consciousness by putting itself into active relation to the world about it, the image that appears to us is impressive. We see a soul, imprisoned in darkness, striving to come to the light, to come to birth, to grow at the expense of an environment that has not been prepared for such a grandiose event. We find ourselves in the presence of a soul engaged in this difficult task, and we do not know how to help it; we may even hinder it.

But even if we confine ourselves to the most elementary and self-evident ideas, we may divine in the baby a play of instincts governing not only its physical but also its psychic functions, as we see in the new-born young of mammals when all at once, by an inward event, they express the characteristics of their race. The human child, indeed, is slower to develop its powers of movement than the young of beasts. While the sense organs are active from birth, and the baby is at once sensible to light, sound, contacts, it has little power of movement. It cannot raise itself, it cannot walk or speak. It lies helpless longer than any other creature, it begins to walk after a year, with great effort, and only after what may be a prolonged period of abortive attempts. It will have learned to walk properly only when it is two. With speech it is the same as with movement. For a long time the child is incapable of articulation; at six months it is just beginning to utter syllables. It is an inert creature, able to scream but not to speak, whereas new-born animals have already their characteristic utterance. Their voice is indeed faint and plaintive, but puppies emit a real bark, kittens miaow, and lambs bleat; in a word, they all have their language, not merely screams and tears like the children of men, the only dumb creatures among all.

It would be a great mistake to think that it is muscular weakness that prevents a baby from standing or sitting upright, or that an incapacity for co-ordinated movement is innate in the human being. The muscular strength of newborn babies as proved by the thrusts or resistance of their members cannot be questioned. And nothing could be more perfect than the difficult co-ordination of sucking and swallowing which they achieve from the first. Nature conditions the child otherwise than the young of animals. She leaves the realm of movement free from the imperious despotism of instinct. Instinct withdraws; the muscles wait, strong and obedient, for a new order; they await the command of the will to co-ordinate them in the service of the human spirit. They must express the characteristics not of a mere species, but of an individual soul. The instincts of the species are also indubitably present, and will impose certain fundamental characteristics: we know that all normal children will walk upright and speak. But each child may reveal such unsuspected individual variations as to constitute an enigma. With every young animal we know what it will be like when it is fully grown; it will be swift-footed if it is a fawn; it will move slowly and heavily if it is an elephant; it will be fierce, with strong jaws, if it is a tiger; it will be gentle and feed on fresh plants if it is a rabbit. There will be no change or inversion in such characteristics. But man is capable of anything. His apparent inertia prepares the surprises of individuality. His inarticulate voice will one day speak, but we do not know in what language. He will speak the tongue that he has picked up by listening to those about him, and with great effort he will form the sounds, the syllables, and finally the words. He will be the personal constructor of all his functions in relation to his environment; he will be the creator of his new being.

This animation of his organs of movement is thus the functional *incarnation* of an individual with characteristics of his own.

That which is commonly known as the flesh is the *complexus* of the organs of motion, known to physiology as the voluntary muscles. As their name implies, they can be moved by the will. Nothing could better indicate that movement is bound up with psychic life. But without its organs, its instruments, the will could do nothing.

Even the instincts of the animals, whatever their species, even those of the smallest insects, could not find expression without organs of movement. In a highly evolved form like that of man, the muscles are infinitely complex, and so numerous that students of anatomy say, "to remember all the muscles, you must have forgotten them seven times." In their functions they combine for the execution of most complicated actions. Some provide impulses, others inhibitions, some are able only to move forward, others only to move back. And yet, with all their opposing functions, they do not act in contradiction but in harmony. Every impulse is corrected by an inhibition, which, therefore, always accompanies it; to each that moves forward is united one that moves back. They are real societies, groups united in single movements, and thus movement is capable of infinite refinements, as for example, in a dancer, in the hand of a violinist, who can transmit infinitesimal movements to the bow of his instrument. Every movement is an association of opposites, every refinement calls for what is almost an army of muscles, acting simultaneously with a.1 opposing army, and in either case perfection is achieved through a time of preparation.

If this preparation is not wholly left to nature, but if a part, indeed, the highest part, implying direction and construction, is entrusted to an individual energy, that energy superimposed on nature is supranatural;

here is the first fact that we must consider in man. There is, in fine, an animating human spirit that must become incarnate in order to act, to express itself in the world. This is the first chapter of the life of the child, man's first task.

If there is an individual incarnation directing the psychic development of the child, the child must possess a psychic life antecedent to its life of motion, existing before and apart from any outward expression. Hesitant and delicate, it appears at the threshold of consciousness, setting the senses in relation to their environment, and immediately acting through the muscles in the effort to find expression. There is an interplay between the individual, or rather between the spiritual embryo, and its environment, and by this interplay the individual forms himself, completes himself. This primordial, formative activity may be compared to the function of the pulsing vesicle that represents the heart in the physical embryo, and which impels nutriment to all parts of the embryonic body, while it itself receives the infiltrations from the blood-vessels of the mother, its vital environment. Thus the psychic individuality develops and organises itself round the action of this motive-principle in relation with the outside environment. The child strives to assimilate his environment and from such efforts springs the deep-seated unity of his personality. This prolonged and gradual labour is a continual process through which the spirit enters into possession of its instrument. It must continually maintain its sovereignty by its own strength, lest movement give place to inertia or become uniform and mechanical. It must continually command, so that movement, removed henceforth from the guidance of a fixed instinct, shall not lose itself in chaos.

Hence a creation that is always in process of realisation, an energy always freshly constructive, the unceasing labour of spiritual incarnation. Thus the human personality forms itself by itself, like the embryo, and the child becomes the creator of the man, the father of the man.

# 3

# Mind in the Making

The sensibility of the very young baby, before it has animated its instruments of expression, leads to a primary mind fabric, which may remain unapparent.

There is something mystical in the idea that the tiniest baby has its mental life. It might lead us to contemplate the new-born infant in the same spirit as that in which in religion we contemplate the Child Jesus, as the incarnation of a God truly present in the tiny body. So, we might imagine, is a human soul, hidden in the tender, helpless body of a baby, a soul already developed and sensible, albeit dumb.

But this conception is not a true one. It would be the same as saying that the new-born child has already within itself a fully formed language, but that the motor organs of speech are as yet impotent to express it. What exists is a predisposition to construct a language. And something of the same holds good in respect of the whole psychological *cormplexus* of which language is the outward manifestation. The baby has a creative aptitude, a potential energy that will enable it to build up a mental world from the world about it. In this it will be exposed to hindering encounters, to a struggle for mental existence, which though unconscious is none the less real, with inexorable consequences as regards the final success of its achievement. If no one helps it, if an environment is not prepared to receive it, it is a creature in continual peril from the point of view of its psychic life. The little child is, we might say, exposed, a waif in the world.

In the course of its psychological development the baby achieves things so marvellous as to be miraculous, and it is only habit that makes us indifferent spectators. How does such a child, come forth from nothing, orient itself in this complicated world? How does it come to distinguish one thing from another, and by what prodigy does it succeed in learning a language in its detailed particularity without a teacher, simply by living? It lives with simplicity and joy, without wearying, whereas a grown-up person who has to orient himself in a new environment needs so much assistance, and to learn a new language must work hard, and even so will never attain the perfection with which he speaks the mother tongue he learned in infancy.

Only recently has it been possible for us to ask ourselves on what does such development depend, and how does a living creature grow.

When we speak of development, of the growth of consciousness, we speak of a fact that is outwardly apparent, but only recently have we come to know anything of its inner mechanism. Modern science has facilitated such investigations in two ways. The one is by the study of the endocrine glands, which affect growth, the discovery of which aroused an immediate and widespread interest in view of their immense practical influence on the care of children. The other is the study of the *sensitive periods* which throws great light on psychic development.

It was the Dutch scientist Hugo de Vries, who discovered the existence of sensitive periods in animal life, but we ourselves, in our schools and by observing the life of children in their families, were the first to discover the sensitive periods of infancy, and to respond to them from the standpoint of education.

These periods correspond to special sensibilities to be found in creatures in process of development; they are transitory and confined to the acquisition of a determined characteristic. Once this characteristic has evolved, the corresponding sensibility disappears. Thus every characteristic is established by the help of an impulse, of a transient sensibility which lasts over a limited period of growth, that is, during the corresponding sensitive period.

Growth is thus not something vague, an inexorable innate heredity, but a labour guided meticulously by transitory instincts which bring an urge to determined activities, and these often differ strikingly from those of the same individual at an adult stage.

In biology these periods were first studied by De Vries, and are particularly apparent in living creatures that reach their adult state through metamorphoses, as in the case of insects. We may take, for instance, the butterfly caterpillar. It must feed on very tender leaves, and yet the butterfly lays its eggs in the most hidden fork of the branch, near the trunk of the tree. Who will show the little caterpillars hidden there, the moment they leave the egg, that the tender leaves they need are to be found at the extreme tip of the branch, in the light? Now the caterpillar is strongly sensible to light; light attracts it, summons it as by an irresistible voice, fascinates it, and the caterpillar goes wriggling towards where the light is brightest, till it reaches the tip of the branch, and thus finds itself, famished for food, among the budding leaves that can give it nourishment. It is a strange fact that when the caterpillar has passed through its first stage and is full grown, it can eat other food, and then it loses its sensibility to light. This has been proved in scientific laboratories where there are neither trees nor leaves but only the caterpillar and the light. The caterpillar will wriggle rapidly towards any ray of light that comes through a hole in the dark box in which it has been enclosed for the experiment. After a certain period, rays of light leave it completely indifferent. This instinct no longer functions. The caterpillar goes other ways, seeks other means of life.

A like active sensibility all at once transforms the caterpillar, once so greedy in its destruction of fine plants, into a kind of fasting fakir. Fasting rigorously, it builds a sort of sarcophagus in which it will remain as though lifeless and this labour is intense and irresistible. So entombed, it will prepare the final phase, the butterfly with its beauty and bright wings.

It is well known that in the grubs of the bee there is a period in which all the females could become queens. But the community chooses one among their number, and for her alone the worker bees make a food substance called by zoologists "royal jelly", which she greedily devours. Thus the privileged bee, by her royal banquets, becomes the queen of a community. If, when a certain time has passed, the bees wished to choose another female grub and were to feed it on the finest royal jelly, it could never become a queen, the period of intense hunger has passed, and its body is no longer capable of such development.

These facts may guide us to an understanding of the crux of the question, even where the human child is concerned. The great difference lies between an animating impulse leading to the performance of wonderful, staggering actions, and an indifference that brings blindness and inaptitude. The adult can do nothing from the outside that will affect these different states.

The child makes a number of acquisitions during the sensitive periods, which place him in relation to the outer world in an exceptionally intense manner. Then all is easy; all is eagerness and life, every effort is an increase of power. But when some of these psychic passions die away, other flames are kindled and so infancy passes from conquest to conquest, in a continuous vital vibrancy, which we have called its joy and simplicity. It is through this lovely flame that burns without consuming that the work of creating the mental world of man takes place.

Thus the exalting vitality of the child explains the miracles of natural conquest to be observed in psychic growth.

Thus what we have called "incarnation" and the sensitive periods might be compared to a spy-hole opening on the inner processes of mind in the making, so that we see, as it were, internal organs at work, determining the mental growth of the child.

It thus becomes clear to us that psychic development does not come about by hazard or does not originate in stimuli from the outer world; it is guided by transient sensibilities, temporary instincts connected with the acquisition of certain characteristics. Though this development takes place by means of the outer world, the latter has no constructive significance. It merely provides the necessary means of psychic life, just as the body, by eating and breathing, takes from its outer environment the necessary means of physical life.

The inner sensibilities we have mentioned determine the selection of necessary things from a many-faceted environment, and of circumstances favourable to development. This guidance is exercised by making the child sensitive only towards certain things, leaving him indifferent towards others. When he is sensible of something, it is as if a light came from him, illuminating that and no other, and of such things his world is made. But it is not a question only of an intense desire to find himself in given situations, or to absorb given elements. The child has a special, unique capacity for profiting by these in order to grow, for it is during the sensitive period that he acquires certain psychological faculties, like that of orienting himself in his outer environment, and becomes able to bring his motor organs to life in all their intimate and delicate particulars.

In these sensitive relations between the child and his environment lies the key to the mysterious recess in which the spiritual embryo achieves the miracles of growth.

We may imagine this marvellous creative activity as a series of keen emotions rising up from the subconscious, which, by contact with the outer world, build up human consciousness. Starting from confusion, they reach distinction, then create activity, as, for example, in the achievement of speech. In the beginning, the sounds of the environment are confusion and chaos, indistinguishable and then, all at once, they are heard as distinct, alluring, fascinating, the separate sounds of an incomprehensible but articulate language, and the mind, as yet without thought, hears a kind of music that fills the world. Then the very fibres of the baby are stirred, not all its fibres, but only those that must now play their part, and which had previously remained hidden, vibrating only in unregulated cries. Now they waken in a regular motion, disciplined, ordered, which changes their manner of vibration, and thus a new rhythm is prepared for the cosmos of the spiritual embryo. But it itself lives intensely in its present and is all concentrated in the present; the glory of its future being remains unknown to it.

Little by little the ear discerns sounds, and the tongue too is animated to new movement; hitherto it merely played its part in sucking, but now it begins to feel an inward vibration and is drawn, as though by an irresistible force, to seek the throat, the lips, the cheeks. These vibrations are life, but as yet they serve no purpose, save to bring an ineffable pleasure.

A sensitive period is at work, a divine command is breathing through helpless things, animating them with the spirit.

This inner drama in a baby's life is a drama of love. Love in its widest sense is the sole great reality, which evolves in the hidden recesses of the soul and from time to time fills it wholly. These marvellous activities do not pass away without leaving indelible traces, by which the man will be the greater, and which give him the higher characteristics that will accompany him all his life; they take place in humble silence.

This is why all happen quietly and imperceptibly, so long as the conditions of the outer environment correspond sufficiently to the child's inner needs. In the case of speech, for instance, which is the hardest of all these processes of animation, and which corresponds to the longest of the sensitive periods, it lies secret because the child is always surrounded by people who speak and therefore provide him with the necessary elements for his achievement. The only outward indication of a baby's sensitive state is its smile, its evident joy when we address it directly in short, clearly pronounced words, so that it can distinguish the sounds as we distinguish a peal of bells. Or we see it grow tranquil in beatific peace, when, of an evening, a grown-up sings a lullaby, using always the same words; it is in such a state of delight that it leaves the conscious world for the world of dreams. It is because we know this, that we talk to the baby with caressing words, to earn its smile, which is so full of life; it is in this knowledge that from time immemorial people have gone of evenings to their babies, who want and demand words and music with the urgency of those asking for comfort on the point of death.

Here are positive proofs of the child's creative sensibility.

But there are other, far more apparent proofs, which have a negative significance. We see them when some external circumstance opposes the child's inward, secret working, bringing violent disturbance and deformation and resulting in defects that will remain throughout life. If the baby has not been able to work in accordance with the guidance of its sensitive period, it has lost its chance of a natural conquest and has lost it for ever.

When something in its environment hinders its inner working, the existence of a sensitive period shows itself by violent reactions, a despair that we believe to be causeless and therefore set down to "naughtiness" and temper. Naughtiness is the expression of an inner disturbance and unsatisfied need, a state of tension; the child's soul is crying out for what it needs, seeking to defend itself.

This shows itself in an increase of useless and restless activity comparable on the physical plane to the high fevers to which babies are liable without any proportionate pathological cause. We know that babies often have alarmingly high temperature with small ailments that would hardly affect the normal state of a grown-up person—and which disappear as quickly as they arise. In the same way, in the psychological field we find violent agitation due to infinitesimal causes, corresponding to a baby's exceptional sensibility. These reactions have always been known, and indeed the tempers small children show almost from birth used to be judged as proofs of the innate perversity of human nature. Well, if every disturbance of function is considered a functional disease, we must call the disturbances that affect the psychic side of life functional disease also. The first "naughtiness" of the baby is the first sickness of the soul.

These violent reactions have been observed because pathological facts are always the first to be noted; it is not tranquillity but the loss of tranquillity that presents itself as a problem demanding thought. The plainest things in nature are not its laws but its aberrations. Thus no one notices the imperceptible outward signs of the creative working of life, or of the functions that subsequently maintain it. The facts of creation and conservation remain hidden. In the functioning of the body the mechanism of the internal organs is something truly wonderful, but no one sees it or notices it. The very individual who lives by them is unaware of their stupendous organisation. Nature works without letting it be known, and we call the harmonious balance of combined energies health, normality. Health! It means triumph in every detail, the triumph of purpose over causes.

We take objective note of all the details of sickness, while the laborious wonders of health may remain unperceived, unknown. It is a fact that in the history of medicine diseases have been known from earliest times. We find traces of surgical treatment left by prehistoric man, while the origins of medicine go back to the civilisations of Greece and Egypt. But the discovery of the functions of the internal organs is very recent. That of the circulation of the blood was made in the 17th century, while the first anatomical dissection of a human body with a view to studying its internal organs took place in 1600. It was pathology, that is to say, disease, that indirectly led to the discovery of the secrets of physiology, that is to say, of normal functions.

It is therefore no wonder that men have been aware only of the psychic maladies of the child, and that the normal working of its soul has remained in complete obscurity. And this is all the more understandable because of the extreme delicacy of such psychic functions, which work in darkness, in secret, without possibility of manifestation.

It is therefore startling but not absurd to say that the adult has known only the diseases of the child psyche, not its health. The healthy psyche remained hidden, like all the forces of the universe yet to be discovered.

If this be so, if we must reckon the baby as among the hidden forces still a secret from us, and if its psychic life develops on a background of functional disharmony and sickness, a vast amount of deformation is bound to result, with blindness, weakness, arrested development. This is not an imaginary picture, but a very present reality. Small causes near the beginnings of life may lead to grave deviation; man grows and matures under a typical aspect other than his own.

## THE CARE REQUIRED

The adult gives no help because he does not even know of the effort the baby must put forth and therefore does not recognise the miracle that is taking place, the miracle of creation from nearly nothing, performed apparently by a being without psychic life.

This conception brings with it a new mode of treating the baby, which has hitherto been considered merely a vegetating little body, with urgent need of physical care but nothing more. To-day what should prevail is an attitude of expectation of the manifestations of mind: in our care of the child we must consider not only what exists but what is still to come. The adult must no longer remain blind to the psychic reality in process of actualisation even in the new-born infant; he must follow its early developments and encourage them. He has not to help the baby to form itself, for this is nature's task, but he must show a delicate respect for its manifestations, providing it with what it needs for its making and cannot procure for itself. In short, the adult must continue to provide a suitable environment for the psychic embryo, just as nature, in the guise of the mother, provided a suitable environment for the physical embryo.

To prove the existence of psychic life in the tiniest child we have no need of scientific experiments, as these are understood by experimental psychology and such as have been attempted by certain modern psychologists who by presenting sensory stimuli to the child try to attract his attention, in expectation of such motor reactions as would indicate a psychic response.

Here, in the first place, is a fact that could not be proved, except at a stage (which may indeed fall within the first year of life), when a psychic co-ordination of the organs of movement has already been achieved, that is to say, when the process of animation or incarnation is in full swing. Whereas there must necessarily be a psychic life, however embryonic, antecedent to any animation of voluntary movement, precisely because it is the psyche that animates such movement.

The earliest form of animation is produced by a feeling. Thus, for example, as Levine has shown in his psychological films, the child who wants something first throws himself upon it with his whole body, and only much later, with the progress of co-ordination of his motor organs, can he separate one action from another, and, for instance, stretch out his hand to take what he wants.

Another example is that of a child of four months, who likes to watch the mouth of a speaker and expresses himself with vague, soundless movements of his lips, but above all by the look of keen attention on his face, that shows him wholly absorbed by the interesting phenomenon before him. None the less, it is only at six months that he begins to pronounce even a syllable. Thus before the earliest articulate utterance, there existed in the child a sensible interest, storing up sounds, secretly preparing the animation of the organs of speech; prior to the act, there was an animating psychic factor. Such sensibilities are subjects for observation, but not for experiment. Indeed such experiments as have been attempted by the experimental psychologists might be among those external circumstances that can damage the secret labour of the infant psyche, calling forth constructive energies before due time.

The psychic life of the baby must be observed as Fabre observed his insects, going in search of them to surprise them in their natural environments, and lying hidden so as not to disturb them. And we must begin with the time in which the senses, like prehensile organs, begin to seize and accumulate conscious impressions of the outer world; for from that moment a life is spontaneously evolving at the expense of its outer environment.

In order to help the child it is not necessary to develop extraordinary powers of observation, or to be able to interpret it. Something much simpler will suffice: it is enough to have a mind prepared to assist the hidden mind of the child. Then common sense will suffice to make us its followers.

The care demanded is both simple and practical, as I will show by a few examples. It is believed, to begin with something very common, that since the baby cannot sit up it must always lie flat. Thus its first sensory relations with its environment must be made with the sky rather than with the earth, but the sight of the sky is just what is withheld from it. In reality it lies looking up at the nursery ceiling, which is usually white and smooth, or at the canopy of its perambulator. And yet it is through sight that the first impressions must be obtained to nourish the hungry spirit.

Those who had a notion that the baby needed something to look at thought of putting objects in front of it, rather than of removing it from the mistaken conditions isolating it from its environment. Acting in the same way as the experimental psychologists, such well-meaning people would tie a string of balls or other coloured objects in front of its cradle. The baby, eager to take in or rather to devour images of its environment follows with its eyes the balls or toys dancing in front of it, twisting itself in an unnatural effort. This deforming effort is forced upon it by an artificial offering, crude in form and movement. It would be enough to put the baby somewhere high, on a slightly inclined plane, so that it could dominate at least the environment of its room. But it could be put in the same way in a garden where the ripple of leaves, flowers, and the leaping and running of animals would form for it a living panorama.

It is necessary that for a long time the scenes of the baby's explorations should be the same. Thus seeing the same things it learns to recognise them, finding them always in the same place, while it learns to distinguish the movements of things moved by the air from the movements of living creatures.

## ORIENTATION THROUGH ORDER

A baby only a month old had never been out of the house. His nurse was holding him on her lap when his father and an uncle living in the house appeared before him *together*. Both men were of more or less the same height and the same age. The baby made a start of intense surprise and almost of fear. The two men stayed in front of him, but separated, one moving to the right and the other to the left. The baby turned to gaze at one of them with plain anxiety, and after a long look at him smiled. But all at once his expression again became anxious,, and more than anxious, frightened. With a swift movement he turned his head to stare at the other, and only after gazing at him for a long time again smiled. He repeated this passage from anxiety to smiles and those movements of his head from right to left quite twenty times before light dawned in his little brain, and he realised that there were *two men.* They were the only men he had seen. Both had made a fuss of him, had nursed him, and spoken affectionate words to him, and he had understood the fact that there was a different kind of being from the many women who surrounded him. He had understood that the world held a different kind of human being from his mother, his nurse, and the various women whom he had had occasion to notice, but never having seen the two men together he had evidently formed the idea that there was only *one* man. Hence his fright when he suddenly realised that the being he had so laboriously catalogued out of chaos had become double.

A characteristic of very small babies is their love of order. Babies of a year and a half or two show clearly something that shows itself obscurely even earlier; they need order in their surroundings. This love of order cannot be compared with that of a good housewife who declares, "I love my home, I love to have it always tidy." She is only talking, but the small baby cannot live in disorder. Disorder disturbs him, upsets him, and he may express his suffering by despairing cries, or by an agitation that can even assume the forms of illness. The small baby is immediately aware of a disorder that grown-ups and even bigger children pass by without perceiving. Order in his outer environment evidently affects a sensibility that vanishes as he grows bigger. It is therefore precisely one of those periodic sensibilities proper to creatures in process of development and which we call "sensitive periods"; it is one of the most important and most mysterious of such periods.

It may seem extraordinary or far-fetched to say that children pass through a sensitive period in regard to external order, when everyone believes that children are untidy by nature. The cause of this contradiction lies in the fact that the baby is unable to show his dispositions in an environment that is not his own, and of which the master is a being stronger than he, namely the adult, who does not understand him, and by his lights considers him a creature of caprice. But how often have we not seen a baby crying desperately, without apparent reason, that is, capriciously? How often have we not seen small babies crying inconsolably? In the soul of the baby there are secrets still hidden from the adult.

But it is only necessary to drop a hint, to give a word of guidance as to the existence of these secret needs, for the adult to become at once aware of them and then he will see how the child soul reveals them.

In our schools, if anything is out of its place, it is the two-year-old child who notices it and puts it back. This does not often happen, because as a rule children of two do not come to school. It is also necessary that children should learn the habit of keeping everything in its place, as happens in our schools where nearly all superfluous objects are eliminated. Moreover, in order to reveal such tendencies, children must have freedom.

A considerable public was able to observe such phenomena as these in our glass school built in the hall of the central building of the San Francisco Exhibition in the year of the opening of the Panama Canal (1917). There was a child of two who, after school, put all the chairs back in their places along the walls. He seemed to be pondering during his work. One day, leaning against a big chair, he seemed uncertain, went away, and then came back and put it a little apart from the others; here indeed was the usual place for the big chair.

Another time, a bigger child, of about four, in pouring water from one receptacle to another, let some drops fall on the floor without noticing it. A tiny child took a rag, sat down on the floor and wiped up the drops as they fell, without the bigger child's paying attention. When the drops of water ceased, the little one asked, "Haven't you any more?" "More what?" asked the bigger one, in surprise.

But if an environment has not been prepared and the baby finds himself among grown-ups, these interesting manifestations, which express themselves so peacefully, may become misery, an enigma, naughtiness.

In order to surprise a positive symptom of this sensibility in small babies, such a symptom as an expression of joy and enthusiasm when their need is satisfied, it is necessary for the adult to have studied this aspect of infant psychology, and, all the more because the sensitive period of order shows itself in the first months of life. Only nurses trained on our principles can give instances of it. I can give an example of a nurse who noticed that as she was wheeling a five-month-old baby in its perambulator slowly through the grounds of its home, it showed special interest and joy at the sight of a white marble tablet inset in a grey, old wall. Though the grounds were full of lovely flowers the little girl always seemed to grow excited and pleased when they came near the tablet. The nurse therefore every day stopped the perambulator in front of it, though it seemed the last thing that could give permanent pleasure to a baby so newly born.

There are, on the other hand, hindrances through which it is easier to perceive the existence of a sensitive period; perhaps the majority of cases of precocious temper arise from such sensibilities.

I will give a few examples taken from real life. Here is a little family scene. The baby in question, only a few months old, was accustomed to lie on a high, oblique bed, so as to dominate its environment. Its room was not the usual white, washable nursery on physically hygienic principles; it was hygienic psychologically. There were coloured panes in the windows, a few pretty pieces of furniture, flowers, and among other things, a table with a yellow tablecloth, on which stood a plant. One day a visitor came in and put her umbrella on the table. The baby girl began to grow excited, and the umbrella was certainly the cause, for after staring at it, she began to cry. It was thought that this meant that she wanted the umbrella, which was brought to her, but she pushed it away. The umbrella was put back on the table, and the nurse gently carried the baby to it, and put her down on the table by the umbrella, but she only cried and struggled the more. The uninitiated would have taken this reaction for one of those precocious fits of temper that show themselves from birth. But the baby's mother, who knew something of a child's early psychological symptoms, took the umbrella from the table and carried it out of the room. Immediately, the child grew calm. The reason for her agitation was that the umbrella on the table was in the wrong place, and this violently disturbed the usual picture of the position of things in an order that the child needed to remember.

Here is another example. The child in this case was much bigger, about a year and a half old, and I myself played an active part in the scene.

I found myself one day with a group of people going through Nero's grotto at Naples. With us was a young mother with a child, too small to be able to walk the whole length of the subterranean passage which goes right through a hill; he seemed about a year and a half old. In fact, after a time, he grew tired, and his mother picked him up, but she had overestimated her strength. She was hot and stopped to take off her coat to carry it on her arm, and with this impediment once more picked up the child, who began to cry, his screams growing louder and louder. His mother strove in vain to quiet him. Indeed, the noise was getting on the nerves of all, and naturally others offered to carry him. He passed from arm to arm, struggling and screaming, and everyone talked to him and scolded him, but he only grew worse.

It looked as if his mother would have to carry him after all, but now he had reached a state of what we call real naughtiness, and the position seemed hopeless. The guide let himself go so far as to exclaim, "Madam, how ever could your husband think of leaving you alone with a child like this? Give him to me!" And he took the child in his sturdy arms with vigorous severity, at which the struggles grew really violent.

I thought of the enigma of infancy, of how reactions must always have a cause, and going up to the mother I said, "Will you allow me to help you put on your coat?" She looked at me in amazement, for she was still hot, but in her confusion she consented and allowed me to help her on with it. At once the baby quieted down, his tears and struggles stopped and he said, "Mamma, coat on." It was as if he wanted to say, "Yes, Mamma, a coat is meant to be worn," as though he thought, "At last you have understood me," and, stretching out his arms to his mother, he came back to her all smiles. The expedition ended in complete tranquillity. A coat is meant to be worn, and not to hang like a rag over one arm, and this disorder in his mother's person had affected the child as a jarring disturbance.

I was present at another family scene that was most illuminating. The mother, who was feeling ill, was sitting, or rather lying, on a sofa, on which the nurse had put two cushions, and her little girl of twenty-one months stood by her asking for a "story". What mother could resist such a plea? Ill as she was, she began a story, the little girl listening with an intent expression. But the mother felt so ill that she could not continue; she had to get up and be helped to bed in a neighbouring room. The child cried, clinging to the sofa, everyone thought it natural for her to cry, from fright and grief at her mother's illness, and they tried to calm her, but when the nurse wanted to take the two cushions from the sofa to carry them into the other room, the child began to scream, "Not cushions, not cushions!" As though she meant, "At least something must stay in its place!"

The child herself was carried with caresses and comforting words to her mother's bed, and her mother, in spite of her illness, made an effort to go on with the story, thinking that thus she would console her. But the child, sobbing, her face bathed in tears, went on repeating, "Mamma, sofa."

The story no longer interested her. Her mother and the cushions had changed their place, the story begun in one room was ending in another, and the conflict in the child's mind was dramatic and irreparable.

These examples show the intensity of the instinct for order, and, what is equally surprising, its extreme precocity. In children in their third year the need for order has entered upon a phase of calm, merging into the active, tranquil period of its applications. Indeed, one of the most interesting things we notice in our schools is that, as we have said, if anything is out of place, it is the child of two who notices it and puts it back. He still feels small details of disorder, which adults or even older children do not notice. If, for instance, a piece of soap is left on the wash-stand instead of in the soap-dish, or a chair is put crooked or in the wrong place, the child of two sees it and goes to put it right. Disorder seems to present an exciting stimulus, an active summons, but it is more than this; to put things tidy brings real enjoyment. Indeed, we notice in our schools that even much bigger children, of three and four, when they have finished a game or exercise put everything back in its place, and this task is plainly as spontaneous and enjoyable as any.

Order—things in their place. It means a knowledge of the arrangement of objects in the child's surroundings, a recollection of the place where each belongs. And this means that he can orient himself in his environment, possess it in all its details. We mentally possess an environment when we know it so as to find our way with our eyes shut, and find all we want within hands' reach. Such a place is essential for the tranquillity and happiness of life.

Plainly the child's *love of order* is something more than what the adult means by the words. It is a vital need at a certain age, in which disorder is painful and is felt as a wound in the depths of the soul, so that the child might say, "I cannot *live* unless I have order about me." It is indeed a question of life and death. For the grown-up it is only a question of external pleasure, of a more or less indifferent comfort. But the child *makes* himself out of the elements of his environment, and this self-making is not accomplished by some vague formula, but following a precise and definite guidance. The guidance of nature enforces its programme and its time-table by a formidable discipline in which health and sickness, life and death play their part. For the tiny child order is like the plane on which terrestrial beings must rest if they are to go forward; it is what water is to the fish. It is necessary that at an early age the child should acquire the *elements of orientation* in the environment in which his spirit must go forward to further conquests.

Peculiarities of this passion for order are revealed in a child's games. Professor Piaget, the Swiss psychologist, who held the post earlier held by Professor Claparede at Geneva, has made interesting experiments with his own children. He would hide something under the cushion of an armchair and then, having sent away the child, transfer it under the cushion of an armchair opposite. His idea was that the child would look for the object, having failed to find it in its original place, and to make the search easier, the professor had put it in a similar hiding place. But the child confined itself to pulling away the cushion from the first chair, saying in his baby language, "It's not there now." The expected response, a search for the vanished object, failed to follow. The professor repeated the experiment, but this time he allowed the child to see him carry the object from one chair to the other. The child, however, repeated the same act as before, with the same comment, "Not there." The professor was about to conclude that his son was stupid, and almost impatiently raised the cushion of the second chair, saying, "Didn't you see me put it here?" "Yes," replied the child, pointing to the first chair, "but it ought to be *here.*"

The child had no idea of looking for anything; this did not concern him, what concerned him was that the thing should return to its place, and perhaps he in his turn concluded that the Professor did not understand the game. Was not the game simply to carry away something and then to put it back in its place? The "hiding" of which his father spoke just meant that the thing was put out of sight under a cushion. But if the thing was not put back, what was the point of the game?

I, too, experienced great astonishment when I began to play with very small children (between two and three years old) at what was meant to be hide-and-seek. In games of this kind children are always keen, happy and highly expectant; so were these. Their game consisted in this: one child, in the presence of the others, hid under a table that was covered by a long tablecloth, then all the others went out, came back, and lifted up the tablecloth with shrieks of delight at the discovery of their playmate hiding underneath. This they repeated again and again. Each one said, "Now I'll hide," and crawled under the tablecloth. Another time I saw much bigger children playing with a little one. They put the little one to hide behind a piece of furniture and, coming back, pretended not to see him and to hunt for him everywhere. Whereupon the little one called out, "I'm here!" with the tone of one who would say, "But didn't you *see* where I was?"

One day I myself joined in such a game. I found a group of little ones shouting for joy and clapping their hands because they had found a playmate hidden behind a door, and they crowded round me, pleading, "Play with us. You hide!" I agreed. They all ran out, just as though they did not want to see where I would go. Instead of going behind the door, I chose a dark corner behind a wardrobe. When the children came back they all ran to look for me behind the door. I waited a little, and then, seeing that they would not look for me, I came out of my hiding-place. The children were all disappointed and downcast. "Why wouldn't you play with us?" they asked reproachfully, "Why didn't you hide?"

If it is true that the aim of a game is pleasure (and indeed these children thoroughly enjoyed repeating their "absurd" rite), we must recognise that at a certain age children take special pleasure in finding things back in the places where they have been put. To hide something means for them to put it somewhere out of sight, where its rediscovery brings a sense of order not only in what can be seen but in what cannot be seen, so that they can say to themselves, "You can't see it, but I know where it is, I can find something with my eyes shut, be sure of the place where it has been put."

Nature gives small children an intrinsic sensibility to order, as built up by an inner sense which is a sense not of distinction between things but of distinction of the relationship between things, so that it perceives an environment as a whole with interdependent parts. Only in such an environment, known as a whole, is it possible for the child to orient himself and to act with purpose; without it he would have no basis on which to build his perception of relationship. It would be like having furniture without a house to put it in. What would be the use of an accumulation of external images without the order that brings them into organised relation? If man knew only separate objects and not their relations, he would find himself in an inextricable confusion. It is to the child's labours that man owes the faculty, which seems a gift of nature of orienting himself, of finding his way about, in the world. In the sensitive period of order, nature gives the first lesson, in the same way as a teacher will show *a* child a plan of the classroom, to prepare him for the study of geographical maps. Or we may say that by this first lesson nature has given man a compass to orient him in the world. In the same way she gives the small child the power of exact reproduction of the sounds that make up language, that language that is capable of infinite development, and which the adult will evolve through the ages. Man's mind does not spring from nothing; it is built up on the foundations laid by the child in his sensitive periods.

## INWARD ORIENTATION

The child's sensibility to order has two simultaneous aspects; the outer, which concerns relations between the parts of his environment, the inner, which gives him a sense of the parts of his body, their movements and position. This latter aspect we may call his inner orientation.

This inner orientation has been the subject of much research. Experimental psychologists speak of a muscular sense which allows the child to become aware of the position of his various members, and which determines a special memory—muscular memory. This explanation has been made the basis of a purely mechanical theory, founded on the experience of conscious movements. If, for example, we move our arm to seize something, we are aware of this movement, memorise and can repeat it.

But the child has proved, on the contrary, the existence of a highly developed sensitive period in respect of the positions of his body long before he can move freely and make any experiments. That is to say, nature prepares a special sensibility towards the aptitudes and positions of the body.

The old theories dealt with the nervous mechanism, but the sensitive periods concern psychological events, spiritual illuminations and vibrations, which prepare the way for consciousness. They are energies starting from non-existence, to bring to existence the basic elements from which the child's psychic world will eventually be constructed. These possibilities originate as a gift of nature, and conscious experiments only develop them further.

We find negative proofs not only of the existence but of the keenness of this sensitive period when in the child's environment circumstances hinder the tranquil evolution of his creative conquests. Then the child falls a prey to acute and often violent agitation, which shows itself not only as temper and crying-fits, but may appear as illnesses which, if the unfavourable circumstances are not removed, defy all attempts at cure; whereas, the moment the obstacle is removed, temper and illness both vanish, a clear proof of the cause of the abnormal phenomena.

An interesting example was reported to me by an English nurse. Since she had to make a short absence from the family who had engaged her, she left in her place an equally skilled nurse to look after the baby. This nurse found her task easy, till it came to bath time. Then the baby became unmanageable. It not only screamed, but struggled to get out of the nurse's arms. The nurse meanwhile took the very greatest care in the preparation of the bath, but in vain. Little by little the baby came to hate the sight of her. When its first nurse came back, it was perfectly good and quiet, and seemed to enjoy its bath. This nurse had been trained on our principles, and was therefore interested in finding the psychological factor, in discovering what enigma of infancy would explain the phenomena that had occurred. With great patience she tried to interpret the imperfect words uttered by a baby at such an early age. She discovered two things. The baby considered the second nurse *naughty*, and why? Because she bathed it the wrong way round. The two nurses, comparing notes, found that whereas the first took the child with her right hand under its head and her left under its feet, the second nurse did the opposite, supporting its head by her left hand and its feet by her right. It thus felt that its head was being put at the end of the bath where it was accustomed to put its feet.

I once found myself involved in a pathological case. I was not called in directly as doctor, but I was a witness to all that happened. A family had just arrived from a very long journey, and one of the children was too small to stand the strain—or rather, that was the opinion of all concerned. Its mother, however, said that on the journey everything had gone smoothly. They had spent the nights at very good hotels, where everything had been prepared for them, with food and a proper cradle for the baby. They were now staying in a comfortable furnished flat; there was no cradle, but the baby slept in a big bed with its mother. Its illness had begun by restlessness at night and digestive troubles. At night it had to be walked up and down, for its screams were thought to come from bowel pains. Specialists had been consulted, and one had prescribed modern foods with a high vitamin content, which were prepared with scrupulous care. Sun-baths, fresh-air treatment, and all the most modern physical methods had failed to give any relief. The baby was growing worse and the nights were despairing vigils for the whole family. Finally, convulsions set in. The baby, when in bed, writhed in alarming spasms. These convulsions began to occur two or three times a day. The baby was still too small to speak, so the greatest aid in knowing its trouble was wanting. It was decided to call a consultation with one of the most famous specialists in nervous diseases of children. It was then that I intervened. The child seemed healthy and, from what its parents said, had been healthy and quiet the whole journey. The cause of its symptoms might therefore be psychological—one of the enigmas of infancy. Then, I had a sudden intuition. The baby was in the big bed, in a fit of agitation. I took two armchairs and set them one in front of the other, so that they made a kind of little bed, walled in by the arms, like a cradle, in it I put blankets and sheets, and without speaking, I dragged it to the side of the bed. The baby looked at it, stopped crying, *rolled over and over* till it reached the edge of the bed, and let itself drop into the improvised cradle, saying, *"Ulla, ulla, ulla!"* [1] And immediately it went to sleep. The symptoms of illness never recurred. It had been protesting, in its way, against a horrible disorder—that of doing away with its bed and putting it in a big bed made for grown-ups.

---

[1] From "culla", Italian for cradle.

Evidently the baby was sensible to the contact of a small bed, enveloping its body, and giving support to all its members, while the big bed gave it no such shelter. The result was a disorder in its inner orientation, and this disorder was the cause of painful conflict, which had brought it into the hands of so many doctors. Such is the power of the sensitive periods. They have the mighty force of creative nature.

The child does not feel order as we feel it; we have already acquired a wealth of impressions and remain indifferent to it, but the child is poor and comes from nothing. In all that he does, he starts from nothing; he knows only the labour of creation, and he leaves us as his heirs. We are like the son of a man who has amassed wealth by the sweat of his brow, and who understand nothing of the struggles and labours that fell to him. We are ungrateful and cold, and adopt an attitude of superiority because we, well provided with everything, have our established place in society. It is enough for us to use the reason that the child developed for us, the will he built up, the muscles he animated that we might use them. We find our way about in the world because he endowed us with the faculty to do so. We feel ourselves because he prepared such a sensibility. We are rich, because we are the heirs of the child, who drew all the foundations of our life from nothing. The child achieved the immense effort of the first step, the step from nothing to a beginning. He is so near to the very founts of life that he acts for the sake of acting, for this is what happens on the plane of creation, and he cannot make himself felt, and he cannot cause himself to be remembered.

## THE UNFOLDING INTELLIGENCE

The child has shown us that his understanding is not something slowly built up from outside. Yet this has been the conception of a mechanistic psychology, which still exercises a major practical influence both on pure science and on education, and thus on the care of the child. Psychologists of this school assert that the images of external objects knock at the doors of sense, and almost force their way in, to be transmitted by an external impulse, till, on the psychical plane, they associate, and, little by little, falling into organised order, build up the mind. This presupposes that the child, from the psychological standpoint, is wholly passive, at the mercy of his environment, and therefore under the complete control of the adult. This idea is completed by another commonly held postulate, that the child from the psychical standpoint is not only passive, but as the old educationists used to say, like an empty vessel, to be filled and moulded.

Our own experiences assuredly do not lead us to underrate the importance of environment in the building up of mind. It is well known how our pedagogy considers the environment so important as to make it the central point of the whole pedagogical approach, while we give to the child's sensorial activity a more fundamental and systematic consideration than any previous educational method. There is, however, a subtle difference between the old conception of the child as passive and the real facts. This difference lies in the existence of the child's inner sensibility. There is a long sensitive period, lasting almost to the age of five, which gives the child a truly prodigious capacity of possessing itself of the images of its environment. The child is an observer who through his senses is actively absorbing images, and this is very different from saying that he is able to receive them like a mirror. To be an observer implies an inner impulse determined by feeling, by special tastes, leading thus to a selection of certain images rather than others. This idea was illustrated by William James when he said that no one ever sees anything in all its details, but everyone sees only a part, determined by his feeling and interests; it is for this reason that various people will give different descriptions of the same thing. Of this, James gives a witty example. If, he says, you are wearing a new suit which pleases you, when you walk along the road you will pay special attention to the clothes of well-dressed people, to such an extent that you risk getting run over.

Now the question arises, what are the interest of the small baby, that will lead it to make a choice from among the infinite medley of images that make up its environment? It is self-evident that the baby will not be affected by interests of an external origin, like those quoted by James, for as yet it has had no experience. The child starts from nothing, it is an active being going forward by its own powers. Let us go straight to the point. The axis round which the internal working of the sensitive period revolves is reason. Such reasoning must be looked upon as a natural, creative function that little by little buds and develops and assumes concrete form from the images it absorbs from its environment.

Here is the irresistible force, the primordial energy. Images fall at once into pattern in the service of reason: it is in the service of his reason that the child first absorbs such images. He is hungry for them, and, we may well say, insatiable. It has always been known that a young child is strongly attracted to light, colours, sounds, in all of which he takes visible delight. But what we want to prove is the inner fact of a reason that exists in a purely germ-state. There is no need for us to underline how we should reverence and assist such passing from nothingness to a beginning; he is bringing into being the most precious gift which gives man his superiority—reason. On this road he goes forward, long before his tiny feet can carry forward his body.

An example is far more illuminating than an argument, so I will recall the very striking one of the child of four weeks already quoted on page 45.

In another environment where the grown-ups concerned had had no idea of the psychical process at work from birth the event would have passed unnoticed, and the baby would have been deprived of the immense help which the two men gave him, by helping him to take a most difficult step, to make an effort towards the actualisation of consciousness.

I should like to add examples taken from much bigger children. There was, for instance, a baby seven months old, who was sitting on the floor playing with a cushion. On the cushion were printed figures of flowers and children, and the little girl, with evident delight, smelled the flowers and kissed the children. An ignorant servant, who was looking after her, interpreted this as meaning that the child liked to play at smelling and kissing everything, so she at once brought her all sorts of things, saying, "Smell this, kiss this." And so the mind which was forming its own patterns, recognising images and fixing them by means of movement, fulfilling an inner constructive labour in joy and tranquillity, was thrown into confusion. Its mysterious labour of inner order was wiped out by the incomprehension of an adult mind.

Adults can thus impede this inner labour, when they fall suddenly upon small children without understanding what these are about, and dance them up and down or try to amuse and distract them. It is the same if they take one of the child's hands and kiss it, as a game, or if they want to make him sleep without paying attention to the psychical process at work in him. The adult, who is unaware of this mysterious

labour, may wipe out the primitive pattern of the child mind, like the
sea when it sweeps over the sand and carries away the sandcastles, so
that those who would build on the sand must begin over and over again.
Whereas it is important that the child should be able to preserve the
images he is-absorbing with a maximum of clarity; for it is through the
clarity and brilliance of impression distinguishing one from the other,
that the ego can build the mind.

A most interesting experience fell to a distinguished child-doctor who
specialised in the artificial feeding of children in their first year of life. He
had founded a large clinic and his researches had shown him that there is
an individual factor to be considered even in feeding; thus not one of the
many milk substitutes can be recommended as "good for children" of a
given age, since a food may be good for one child and bad for another. His
clinic was the most perfect of the kind, from both scientific and aesthetic
standpoints. The results on the health of the children were marvellous, up
to six months old, but after that period, they all went down in health. This
was a mystery, for artificial feeding becomes easy after the first six months.
Now he had, connected with his clinic, a surgery for poor mothers who
could not feed their children, and who thus had need of artificial foods,
given in accordance with the advice they obtained at the clinic. And these
children, unlike those in the clinic, did not grow ill after six months. After
many observations the professor thought that some psychic factor might
explain the phenomenon, and at once he was able to note that the babies
of over six months old were suffering from *boredom, through want of food
for the mind.* He began then to amuse them, to vary their lives, to see that
when they were taken out it was not only on the terrace of the clinic; the
result was that they regained their health.

A vast number of experiments have shown with absolute certainty that
during their first year of life children have acquired their sense impressions
of their environment with such clarity as to recognise them in pictures,
perspective or the flat. But besides this we can affirm that these impressions
are already outgrown and no longer afford a living interest.

From the beginning of their second year of life, children are no longer
drawn, by the peculiar fascination we notice in the sensitive periods, to
showy objects or bright colours, but rather to tiny things that we should
not notice. It is as though what now interests them is the invisible, or
that which lies on the very edge of consciousness.

I noticed this sensibility for the first time in a little girl fifteen months old. I heard her laugh out loud in the garden, in a way unusual in such small children. She had gone out alone and was sitting on the paving stones of the terrace. Near her was a bed of magnificent geraniums, flowering under an almost tropical sun. But the child was not looking at them; her eyes were fixed on the ground, where there was nothing to be seen. Here then was another of the enigmas of infancy. I crept up and looked where she was looking, but saw nothing. It was she who explained to me, in words that were hardly words, "There is something tiny moving down there." With this guidance, I was able to see a tiny, almost invisible insect, the colour of the stone, moving very quickly. What had struck the child was that such a tiny creature could exist, and could move, could run. Her wonder filled her with noisy delight, greater than what is usual in small children. And her joy did not come from sunlight, flowers or colour.

I had a similar experience with another child of about the same age. Her mother had given her a large collection of coloured postcards, and the child seemed anxious to show them to me.

"Bam-bam!" she said. It was her word for a motor-car, and I understood that it was the picture of a car she wanted to show me. There was an abundance of pictures; evidently her mother had sought to combine instruction with pleasure. There were pictures of exotic animals, giraffes, lions, bears, monkeys, birds and there were the domestic animals that would certainly interest a small child—sheep, cats, donkeys, horses, cows—and there were little landscapes that showed animals, houses and people. But the strange fact was that in all that rich collection there was no motor-car.

"I don't see any car," I said. The child hunted through the pack, and pulled out a card, saying triumphantly, "There!" The picture showed a hunting scene, but the chief object was a very fine setter. Further off, in perspective, was the huntsman, with a gun on his shoulder. In a corner, in the distance, was a tiny cottage, with a wavy line that was meant to be a road, and on that line was a black dot. The child pointed to the dot, saying, "Barn-bam." And, in fact, it could just be recognised, in spite of such small proportions, that the dot represented a car. It was the difficulty of seeing it, the fact that a car could be made to look so tiny, that made the picture interesting, and worth showing to me.

I thought that perhaps no one had shown the child the pretty and instructive pictures on the other cards. I chose one, with the head and neck of a giraffe, and began to explain:

"Look, what a funny neck, so long...."

"Affa!" (giraffe), said the child gravely. I had not the courage to go on.

It would seem that there is a period during the second year of life in which nature leads the mind by successive stages to complete apprehension of the things of its environment. I shall give a few examples drawn from my own experience. I once wanted to show a little boy about twenty months old a fine book, which was meant for grown-up people. It was a copy of the Gospels, illustrated by Gustae Doré, who had, here and there, reproduced figures from the Old Masters, such as Raphael's Transfiguration. I chose the picture of Jesus calling the children to Him, and began to explain:

"There is a child right in Jesus' arms, another leaning his head against Him, and they are all looking at Him, and He loves them...."

The child's face did not show the smallest interest, and, pretending not to notice, I turned over the page and began to look through the book for another picture. All at once the child said:

"Sleeps."

The words produced in me a disconcerting realisation of the mystery of the child mind.

"Who sleeps?"

"Jesus," answered the child vigorously, "Jesus sleeps," and he motioned to me to turn back the pages. The figure of Christ was placed high, so that He was looking down on the children, with eyelids lowered, as over sleeping eyes. The child's attention had been drawn to a detail that no adult had remarked.

I went on with my explanation, and stopped at a picture taken from Raphael's Transfiguration, saying, "Look, how Jesus is raised up above the earth, and how people are frightened. Look at the child with its eyes all twisted, and that woman who is stretching out her arms." I realised that my explanation was not really suitable for a child, and I had not made a good choice of pictures. But now what interested me was to evoke another enigmatic response, and almost to compare what an adult sees in so complex a picture with what would be seen by such a very small child. But this time he only made a kind of grunt, as if to say, "Get on," and his little face showed no sign of interest. While I was preparing to turn over the page, he touched a little medallion that he wore round his neck, and which was shaped like a rabbit. Then he said, "Bunny." "He is distracted by his locket," I thought. But then he showed vigorously that he wanted me to turn back the page. And there, sure enough, in the picture of the Transfiguration, was a tiny rabbit, on one side. Who has ever noticed it?

Grown-ups believe that children are sensible only to very showy things, bright colours, loud noises, etc. It is true that such violent stimuli attract their attention; we have all seen children attracted by people singing, the sound of bells, flags flying, or brilliant lights. But such violent attractions from without are only incidental; they distract the attention, awaken it with violence, and disperse it over what has stimulated the senses. We, too, though the parallel is not exact, if we are deep in a book and suddenly hear a loud band beneath the window, get up to go and look. Anyone who did not perceive that a man sitting silently reading is intensely concentrated, and who only saw him get up to listen to the band, would say that men are more stimulated by sound than by anything else. That is how we have judged children. But the fact that a strong external stimulus attracts their attention is incidental, and comes about by chance. It has no relation to the profound, formative part of the child mind, which belongs to his inner life. We may discern the manifestations of this inner process when we find children intent on tiny things, that are scarcely perceptible. Whoever observes the smallness of things takes a great interest in things in themselves, and no longer feels them as sensory impressions but as the expression of an "intelligence of love".

For all practical purposes, the child spirit is a secret from the adults; it appears to them as an enigma; for they judge of it merely from practical impotence in reaction and not from the psychical energy that is potent in itself. We must reflect that behind every manifestation there is a decipherable cause. There is no phenomenon that has not its motives, its *raison d'être*. It is too easy to judge every puzzling reaction, every difficult phase as a whim. Such whims should assume the importance of a problem that must be solved, an enigma that must be deciphered. This is certainly difficult, but extremely interesting; it means above all a new and loftier attitude on the part of the adult. It makes him a student rather than a blind ruler, or a tyrannical judge, such as he is too often in relation to the child.

A group of women with modern ideas were discussing just this problem, in a corner of a drawing-room. Near them, playing quietly by himself, was their hostess' son, a little boy about a year and a half old. The talk passed from theory to more concrete things, and the books written for tiny children were discussed. "They are silly books with absurd pictures," said the young mother. "I have one with me now called *Little Black Sambo*. Sambo is a little nigger boy. On his birthday his parents have given him all sorts of things—an umbrella, a pair of trousers, shoes, stockings and a coloured jacket, and they are preparing a fine dinner for him. Meanwhile Sambo, who wants to show off his new clothes, puts them on, and creeps out of the house. And then he meets various wild beasts, who frighten him, and to appease them he must give away his clothes, piece by piece, so that the giraffe has the umbrella, the tiger the shoes, and so on, till poor little Sambo goes home naked and crying. But his parents forgive him and all ends happily in a grand feast, as you see in the last picture."

The book was handed round. And all at once, the little boy's voice was heard, "No, lola."

Everyone was surprised; here, maybe, was one of the enigmas of childhood. The child had spoken. Indeed he went on vigorously repeating his mysterious assertion, "No, lola."

"Lola," his mother said, "is the name of a nurse he had for a few days." But the child began to scream, calling "lola" in what seemed a fit of unreasonable temper. Then someone brought the book to him, and he pointed to the last picture not in the text, but on the back of the cover, showing a little nigger in tears. At once all understood. By "lola" he was saying, in his baby language, the Spanish word *"llora"*, which means, "cries."

The fact was this; the end of the book was not the happy banquet, but the picture on the back of the cover of Little Black Sambo crying. No one had noticed that this picture was there. The little boy was making a logical protest, because his mother had said, "It all ends happily." For him, it was plain that the book ended with Sambo crying. He had observed the book more attentively than his mother, and he was accurate and original in deciding that this was the last picture. But what was still more striking was that while he was barely able to articulate a single word, he could follow the whole drift of a long conversation.

It is evident that there are two different personalities in the child and the adult. It is not a case of a minimum growing gradually to a maximum.

Children, who see the smallest details of things in their reality, must look upon us, who project our own mental synthesis into what we see, as inferior creatures, incapable people who do not know how to look at things. Perhaps to their judgment we have no sense of accuracy, and, moreover, pass over interesting things with indifference, or unconsciousness. Assuredly, if they could express themselves, they would reveal that in the depths of their mental world they have no confidence in us, just as we have no confidence in the child, who is alien to our mode of conceiving things. That is why the grown-up and the child do not understand each other.

# 4

# Where Adults Hinder

### THE QUESTION OF SLEEP

The conflict between the grown-up and the child begins when the child has reached a point where he can do things on his own.

Earlier no one can wholly prevent the child from seeing and hearing, that is, from making a sensory conquest of his world. And the grown-up who is aware of the existence of an intense, psychic life in the child is ready to make the conditions of his environment more rational, in order to facilitate the process of quiet absorption at work in the child mind.

But when the child grows active, walks, touches things, it is quite another thing. Grown-ups, however much they love a child, feel an irresistible instinct to defend themselves from him. It is an unconscious feeling of fear of disturbance by an unreasoning creature, combined with a proprietary sense where objects are concerned that might be dirtied or spoiled.

This complex, anxious, defensive attitude conflicts with the love by which the grown-up believes that the child's presence gives him the greatest joy, and that he himself is ready to make every sacrifice, in utter self-surrender. Now the two psychological states, that of the grown-up and that of the child, are so different, that it would be almost impossible for the child and the grown-up to live together unless necessary adjustments were made. Here lies the grave problem of how the child should be treated in the bosom of his family.

It is easy to see that these adjustments will be to the complete disadvantage of the child, who is in a state of utter social inferiority. The repression of inconvenient acts on the part of the child in the environment where the adult reigns, becomes inevitable through the fact that the adult is not conscious of his own defensive attitude, and is conscious only of love and generous self-surrender. The camouflage of which Freud speaks comes precisely from such conflicts. The subconscious instinct of defence appears consciously in another guise; the proprietary sense that makes the adult anxious to defend things he cherishes from the child becomes at once, "the duty of training the child so as to teach him good habits," and fear of the small disturber of his comfort becomes "the need to make the child rest a lot for the good of his health."

A working-class mother, in her simplicity, defends herself openly by slaps, scolding and abuse, and by driving the child out of doors into the street—in the intervals of expansive hugs and smacking kisses, which correspond to the part of her that is full of love for her child.

In a higher grade of society, where certain forms of feeling, such as love, sacrifice, duty, control in outward acts, are taken for granted, such instincts must be camouflaged. But upper-class mothers are even readier than mothers of the people to rid themselves of their children by confiding them to a nurse, who will take them out and make them spend long hours in sleep.

The patience, niceness, and indeed submissiveness of upper-class mothers to the nurses they employ are really a tacit understanding that they will forgive anything, bear anything, so long as the disturbing child is kept away from his parents and from their possessions.

And thus it is that the child has barely emerged from imprisonment in a helpless body, and is rejoicing in the triumph of his ego now animating those marvellous instruments of activity, the organs of voluntary movement, when he is met by a mighty host of giants who impede his entry into the world. Here is a situation that reminds us of the exodus of a primitive people, seeking to free itself from slavery, and advancing through inhospitable and unexplored lands, like the Jewish people under the leadership of Moses. When they had at last left behind the wastes of the wilderness and had found a fertile oasis where they might live at peace, they found not hospitality but war.

Human nature is such that those who possess an established environment will defend themselves against invaders. This shows itself plainly and violently in the case of conflicting peoples, but the source of such phenomena lies hidden in the subconscious depths of the human soul. And its first manifestation, which has passed unperceived, is found when the adult world defends its peace and its possessions against the invading people of the new generations. But the advance of the invaders is not arrested; they fight desperately, for they are fighting for life.

Such a conflict, subconscious, camouflaged, takes place between the child's innocence and his parents' love.

\* \* \*

It is very convenient for the grown-up to say, "The child must not run about, must not touch our things, must not talk or shout, must spend a lot of time lying down, must eat and sleep." Or else to decide that it "is best" for the child to be sent away from home, even among persons without affection and unconnected with the family. The adult, by force of inertia, takes the easiest path, and puts the child to sleep.

Who would deny that a child needs sleep? But if a child is so alert, so capable of observation, he is not primarily a sleeper. He will need normal sleep, and we must certainly see that he gets it. But we must distinguish between normal sleep and sleep artificially provoked. We know that a strong-willed person can impose suggestion on a person of weaker will, and that the first step in suggestion lies in putting the patient to sleep. It is thus the adult who by use of suggestion, albeit unconsciously, sends the child to sleep.

Uneducated mothers openly give their children sleeping-draughts, peasants will know how to prepare certain decoctions of poppy heads to make their babies sleep for long periods. But apart from this, we may say that grown-ups in general, cultured or uncultured, and even specialised in the care of children, such as nurses, agree in condemning these living beings to sleep when nature would have them wake. Not only small babies a few months old, but bigger children, of two, or three, or four, are forced to sleep far more than they need. In the latter case, this does not apply to children of the people. They spend all day playing in the streets, so that they do not worry their mothers, and are thus spared this danger. And it is a well-known fact that children of the people are *less nervous* than those higher in the social scale. And yet people insist on "long sleeps" as necessary for the health of children, like eating and fresh air; they are concerned only with what we may call the vegetative life of the child. I remember a little boy of seven who confided to me that he had never seen the stars because he had always been put to sleep before nightfall. "I should like," he told me, "just one night to go to the top of a mountain and lie down on the ground to look up at the stars." Many parents boast that they have so accustomed their children to go to sleep early that they themselves are absolutely free to go out for the evening.

The beds prepared for children once they are able to run about are something quite special. They are not like the cradle, which has a certain beauty of form and is soft, or like the beds of grown-ups, made simply so that the children may sleep comfortably. A child's cot is a cruel prison prepared for this creature that is fighting for psychic existence. In it, the child is a prisoner, and the iron cage into which he is lowered unwillingly is at once a reality and a symbol. He is the prisoner of a civilisation that has been built up by adults for the good of adults; and which tends to grow more and more restrictive and to leave less and less room for the freedom of the child. Around the child there are only prison and emptiness.

The child's cot is a cage on high supports, so that the grown-up can handle the child without stooping, and so that he can leave the child alone, sure, that though he may cry, he cannot hurt himself. The room is darkened so that no light, not even the light of dawn, may shine to waken him. The child must go to sleep early in the evening so as to leave his parents free, and he must sleep late in the morning till they have had the sleep necessary for grown-ups who have gone to bed late.

One of the first ways of helping the psychological development of the child is a reform of his bed and of the custom of constraining him to unnaturally long sleep. The child should have the right to sleep when he is sleepy, to wake when he has slept enough, and to get up as soon as he likes. We therefore advise—and many families have taken our advice—that the old child's cot should be done away with, and that in its place a very low bed should be made, which the child can enter or leave when he likes. This simple little reform will solve many difficulties that seemed hard of solution. A little, low bed, almost on the floor, is economical, like all reforms that will assist the child in his mental life, for the child needs simple things about him, and instead the few things existing for his sake have been complicated in a manner detrimental to him. In many families this reform has been achieved by putting a little mattress on the floor, on a big, soft carpet, with the result that children go to bed of themselves, and say good night gaily, and in the morning get up without waking anyone. There are many examples that go to show how profound a mistake has been made in the ordering of a child's life, and how the grown-up, anxious to do what is good for the child, really goes counter to his needs, and, unconsciously, is moved by a defensive instinct which could easily be overcome.

From all this it follows that the adult should try to interpret the child's needs and meet them as best as he can by preparing a really suitable environment. This may be the beginning of a new epoch in education, which will consider how it can *assist the life* of the child. We must finish with the idea that the child is an object to be picked up and carried anywhere when he is small, and that when he is bigger he must simply obey and imitate the adult. This idea is an insuperable obstacle to any endeavour to make the child's life more rational. The adult must recognise that he must take second place, endeavour all he can to understand the child, and to follow and help him in the development of his life. This should be the aim of mother and teacher. If the child's personality is to be helped to develop, since the child is the weaker, the adult with his stronger personality must hold himself in check, and, taking his lead from the child, feel proud if he can understand and follow him.

## DELIGHT IN WALKING

It should be the adult's task to correspond to the needs of the immature creature in his care, to adapt himself to its necessities, and to renounce his own manner of action.

The higher animals instinctively do something of the sort, and adapt themselves to the conditions of their little ones. There is nothing more interesting than what happens when a baby elephant is brought by its mother into the herd. The great mass of huge animals slows its pace to the pace of the little one and when the little one is tired and stops, all stop.

There are also certain forms of civilisation into which the idea of such sacrifices for the child has entered. I once watched and followed a Japanese father who was taking his little son about a year and a half old for a walk. All at once the little one clasped his father's leg. The father stood still, so that the child could go round and round the leg he had chosen for his game. When the child had had enough, the slow walk went on. After a little while, the child sat down on the edge of the pavement, and his father stood still beside him. The father's face was grave and natural; he was not doing anything out of the ordinary, he was simply taking his child for a walk.

This is how a child should be taken out so that he may practise the essential act of walking at a time when his organism requires to establish the variety of co-ordinated movements that will give him balance. We must realise the immense difficulty, reserved for human beings alone, of walking upright on only two feet.

Though a man's body is formed of members that correspond to those of other mammals, he must walk on two feet instead of four. Even monkeys have long arms that enable them to rest a hand on the ground when they walk. Man alone must entrust to two limbs the whole task of balanced walking, instead of walking with support. When mammals walk they lift two feet, diagonally, so that their bodies have always two supports, but man as he walks rests his weight first on one foot, then on the other. This difficulty is indeed solved by nature but by two means, of which the one is instinct, the other voluntary individual effort.

The child does not develop the power to walk upright by waiting for it, but by walking. The first step, greeted with such joy by his family, is indeed a conquest of nature, and almost the birth of active man, in place of inert, helpless man, and for the child a new life begins. In physiology, the emergence of this new function is one of the main tests of normal development. But afterwards, it is practice that counts. The achievement of balance and sure footing is the result of long practice and hence of individual effort. We know that the child starts walking with an irresistible impetus and courage. He is bold, even rash; he is a soldier who hurls himself to victory regardless of risk. And for this reason the adult surrounds him with protective restrictions, which are so many obstacles; he is enclosed within a play-pen, or strapped in a perambulator, in which he will make his outings even when his legs are already sturdy.

This happens because a child's step is much shorter than that of a grown-up, and he has less staying-power for long walks. And the grown-up will not give up his own pace. Even when the grown-up is a nurse—that is to say, someone who has specialised and given herself up to a child's sole care—it is the child who must adapt himself to the ways of the nurse, not the nurse to him. The nurse will go her own pace, pushing the perambulator in which the child sits like some fine fruit being driven to market. And only when the nurse has reached the place for which she is aiming, perhaps a pleasant park, will she sit down, and let the child get out to play under her watchful eye. In all this, only the child's body is considered, his "vegetative" life, which must be shielded from any possible external danger, but no account is taken of the essential and constructive needs of his mental life.

Between the age of a year and a half and two the child can really walk quite a mile and he can negotiate difficult places, steep rises or stairs. But he walks with quite a different aim from our own. The grown-up walks to reach an external goal, and he goes straight towards it. He has, moreover, his own rhythm of walking, which carries him forward almost mechanically. The small child walks to develop his powers, he is building up his being. He goes slowly. He has neither rhythmic step nor goal. But things around him allure him and urge him forward. If the adult would be of help, he must renounce his own rhythm and his own aim.

In Naples I knew a young family of which the smallest child was eighteen months old. In summer to reach the sea they had to walk nearly a mile on a precipitous road down the hill, which was almost impracticable for any sort of conveyance. The young parents wished to take the baby with them, but to carry him would have been too tiring. The child himself solved their difficulty by showing he could walk the whole way. Every now and then he would stop to look at a flower, or sit down on the grass of a meadow, or stand to watch an animal. Once he stood for about a quarter of an hour watching a donkey grazing. And so, every day, this baby went down and up the long difficult road and was not overtired.

In Spain I knew two children between two and three years old, who went for walks of over a mile. Other children would spend over an hour in going up and down steep stairs with very narrow steps.

Speaking of stairs, I am reminded that here again is a cause of accusation of "naughtiness" from anxious mothers. A lady once asked me about the fits of temper revealed by her little girl who could just walk. The child screamed whenever she saw a flight of steps, and when she was lifted to be carried up or down them she became a little fury. Her mother thought that this was merely a coincidence, for there seemed no reason for the child to cry and struggle just because she was being carried up or down the stairs. But it was plain that the little one wanted to go up and down the stairs *by herself.* They clearly seemed to her most attractive places, with so many holds for her hands and all made up of little seats, far more alluring to walk on than the fields, where her foot sank in the grass and her hands had nothing to which to cling. But the fields were the only places where she was allowed to move about without being held in the arms of a grown-up, or shut in a perambulator.

It is easy to notice how children want to walk and run; and how a flight of steps in the open will always be full of children going up and down, sitting down, getting up, sliding. The ability of the little street urchin in finding his way in and out of obstacles, avoiding dangers, running, and even hanging on to moving carts, shows a potentiality very far removed from the inertia of the timid and eventually lazy child of the upper classes. Neither has *been helped* in his development; one has been abandoned to the unsuitable and dangerous environment in which the grown-up lives, the other, to save him from this dangerous environment, has been repressed, and hedged in by protective obstacles.

The child struggling to build up the man in him is like the Messiah, of whom the prophets said that He had no place to lay His head or move His feet.

## HAND AND BRAIN

It is interesting to note that the two great landmarks which physiology regards as signs of the normal development of a child have both to do with movement. They are the beginning of walking and the beginning of speech. Science, therefore, has considered these two motor functions a kind of horoscope in which to read the future of the man; for indeed these two complex manifestations show that the man-to-be has won the first victory of his ego over his instruments of expression and activity. Now language is specifically characteristic of man, for it expresses thought, while walking is an action common to the animals. An animal differs from a vegetable in that it can move about by itself, and when this movement is entrusted to special limbs, walking becomes a basic characteristic. But in man, though his power of moving his body in space is so great as to have led to his invasion of the whole earth, walking is not his specifically characteristic movement as an intelligent being.

Instead, the true "motor characteristics" connected with mind are the movements of the vocal organs in language and those of the hand in the service of the mind in working out an idea. We know that the first traces of man in prehistoric eras are deduced from the presence of the chipped and polished stones that were his first tools. This then is the characteristic that cuts a new furrow in the biological story of living creatures. Language itself appears as a document of man's past when it, a sound that is lost in air, has become something man's hand has engraven on stone. The morphology of the body and the achievement of walking are characterised by this liberation of the hand, the dedication of the upper limbs to other functions than those of mere movement, so that they become the executive organs of the mind. It is thus that in the evolution of living beings man takes up a new position, revealing the functional unity of his psyche and movement.

The hand is the delicate and structurally complicated organ that allows the mind not only to manifest itself but to enter into special relations with its environment. Man, we may say, takes possession of his environment by his hand and transforms it as his mind directs, thus fulfilling his mission on the great stage of the universe.

It is therefore logical, when we wish to judge of the psychological development of a child, to consider the first beginnings of what we may call the two forms of mind-inspired movement, the appearance of speech and the appearance of activity in the hand, as aspiring to work.

By subconscious instinct man has always associated these two motor manifestations of the mind, peculiar to the human race, and has recognised their significance, but only in certain symbols connected with the social life of the adult. For instance, when a man and woman marry they utter certain words and join their hands. To consent to marry is "to give one's word" and to ask a woman in marriage is to "ask her hand." In an oath a word is spoken and a gesture is made. In any ritual into which expression of the ego enters strongly, the hand plays its part. Pilate, to show his repudiation of all responsibility, declares in the ritual phrase that he washes his hands, and at the same time actually washes his hands before the crowd. The Catholic priest during Mass, before entering upon the most intimate part of the sacred function, announces that he will wash his hands, "I will wash my hands among the innocent," and washes them in a little basin, though his hands were not only washed but purified before he went up to the altar.

All this shows how in the subconsciousness of humanity the hand is felt to express the inner "I". Can we conceive of anything more sacred or more wonderful than the development of this essentially human movement in the child? Nothing should awaken more solemn expectancy. The first stretching out of those tiny hands towards things, the impetus of a movement that represents the effort of the ego to penetrate the world, should fill the adult observer with wonder and reverence. And instead, man is afraid of those tiny hands as they stretch out to the valueless and insignificant objects within their reach; he sets out to defend these objects against the child. He is constantly repeating "Don't touch!" just as he repeats, "Sit still! Be quiet." And in this anxiety, in the shadowy deeps of his subconsciousness, he organises a defence, calling on the assistance of other men, as though they must secretly fight against a power that threatens their comfort and their goods.

To see or to hear, that is, to garner from its environment the elements necessary to build up its first mental fabric, the child must be able to take possession of them, to "grasp" them. Now when the child has to move in a constructive manner, using his hands at some work, he needs to have outward things that he can handle, that is, it is necessary for him that "motives of activity" should exist in his environment. But in his home this need has not been considered. The things that surround him all belong to grown-ups and are made for their use. They are forbidden to the child—tabooed. The command "Don't touch!" is the only answer to this vital problem of infant development. If the child touches such forbidden objects, he is punished or scolded. If he succeeds in taking hold of something, he is like a hungry little puppy who carries off a bone to gnaw it in a corner, trying, insufficient as it is, to find nourishment in it, before he is chased away.

Now the child's movements are not due to chance. He is building up the necessary co-ordinations for organised movements directed by his ego, which commands from within. The ego, organising and co-ordinating, is bringing his inner psyche and his organs of expression into unity by means of continual integrative experiences. It is, therefore, important that the child himself, acting spontaneously, should choose and execute his acts. Such formative movement has special features; it is not the result of disordered or chance impulses. It is not just running, or jumping, or handling things aimlessly, or simply displacing them so as to create disorder, or destroy them. Constructive movement finds its inspiration in actions that the child has seen performed by others. The actions he tries to imitate are always those that mean the handling or the use of something, with which the child tries to perform the actions he has seen performed by adults. Therefore these activities are associated with the usages of his various domestic or social surroundings. The child will want to sweep and wash up, or wash clothes, pour out water, or wash and dress himself, brush his own hair. Since this is a universal fact, it has been called imitation: the child does what he has seen done. But there is a difference between what he does and the direct imitation we associate with a monkey. The child's constructive movements start from a psychical structure, built up on an apprehension. His psychical life, which must govern his movements, is always pre-existent to the movements associated with it. When the child wants to do something, he knows beforehand what it is; he wants to do something that he knows, that is, that he has seen done. We may say the same about the development of speech. The baby absorbs the speech it hears spoken around it, and when it says a word it says it because it has learned it by hearing it, and holds it present in the memory. It uses it according to its need of the moment. This knowledge and use of a word it has heard is not imitation in the sense that a parrot's talk is imitation. It is a case not so much of immediate imitation as of something that has been observed and stored up, of knowledge that has been acquired. Its reproduction as speech is a distinct act. This distinction is very important because on the one hand it throws light on the relations between an adult and a child, and on the other it allows us a more intimate comprehension of child activities.

## PURPOSEFUL ACTIVITY

Before the child can perform actions with a clearly logical motive, such as those he has seen performed by grown-ups, he begins to act for purposes of his own, using things for ends that are often unintelligible to adults. This often happens with children between a year and a half and three. Once, for example, I saw a child of a year and a half who found a pile of napkins that had just been ironed and were neatly laid one on top of the other. The child took one of these folded napkins, holding it with the greatest care and putting one hand under it so that it should not unfold, and carried it diagonally across the room to the opposite corner, where he put it on the ground saying " One!" He then went back, taking the same diagonal path—a sign that he was guided by some special directional sensibility. He took a second napkin in the same way, carried it along the same path, and put it down on the top of the first, saying again "One!" This he did till he had carried over the whole pile. Then, in exactly the same fashion, he took them all back to their original place. Although the pile of napkins was no longer in the perfect state in which the maid had left it, all the napkins were still fairly well folded, and though the tower they made showed certain deficiencies, it could not be considered dismantled. Luckily for the child no one of the family had been present during the lengthy manoeuvre. How often do small children see a grown-up descending on them with a cry of "Stop! Put that down!" And how many times are those tiny, so much to be venerated hands, slapped so that they shall learn not to touch things!

Another "elementary" occupation that fascinates children is to take stoppers in and out of bottles, especially if the stopper is one of prismatic glass, reflecting the colours of the rainbow, like that of a scent bottle. This unstoppering and restoppering of bottles seems one of their favourite elementary movements; another is to raise and lower the top of a big ink-stand or the lid of a massive box, or to open and shut the door of a cupboard. And it goes without saying that there will often be war between the grown-up and the child over these too alluring objects which are so eminently tabooed because they belong to mamma's dressing-table or daddy's writing-desk or the drawing-room furniture. And often the result is "naughtiness". But the child does not want just that particular bottle, or that ink-stand; he would be satisfied with *things made for him,* allowing him to practise the same movements.

These and similar actions are primary actions that have no logical purpose, and which can be considered the first stammering steps of man as worker. It is this preparatory period that we have envisaged in some of our apparatus for the use of very small children, such as our solid insets, which have had such universal success.

The idea of leaving the baby free to act is one that is easily understood, but which in practice encounters complicated obstacles deeply rooted in the adult mind. Often a grown-up who will wish to leave the child free to touch and move things will be unable to resist vague impulses which end by mastering him. A young mother in New York had assented to these ideas, and wished to put them into practice with her fine little son, who was two and a half years old. One day she saw him carrying a jug full of water from the bed-room into the drawing-room, for no reason. She saw how tense he was, the effort he was making at every step, while all the time he kept repeating to himself, "Be careful, be careful!" The jug was heavy, and a moment came when his mother could not resist helping him, so that she took the jug from him and carried it to the place he wished. The little boy remained tearful and humiliated, and his mother was grieved to think she had caused him pain. She justified herself by saying that though she knew that he was driven by some inner necessity, she felt she could not let him tire himself out and spend so much time on something she could do for him in a moment.

"I know I did wrong," she told me, asking my advice almost as though she were a sick person asking a doctor how she could be cured.

I pondered on the other side of the question, the instinct to defend things against the child, that feeling almost of avarice where the child is concerned. I asked her, "Have you any rare china, some cups for instance, that are really valuable? Then let him carry one of those light little cups, and see what happens?" She followed my advice and told me afterwards that her little son carried the cups with care and attention, stopping at every step, till he had brought them safely to their destination. The mother was torn between two feelings, her joy in seeing the child at work and her anxiety for the cups. The two feelings counterbalanced each other so that she could make herself allow the child to perform the task that so passionately attracted him and which seemed necessary to his psychic health.

On another occasion I gave a little girl of a year and a half a duster which was a source of delight as she sat down and dusted various shining things. But in her mother there was a kind of inhibition that did not allow her to give a small child something so seemingly futile and so far removed from the hygienic principles she had learned.

The first manifestations of the instinct to work are profoundly disturbing to any adult who has realised their importance. He sees that he must make an immense renunciation; as though he must mortify his personality, surrender his environment, and this is incompatible with social life as it exists. In an adult environment the child is undoubtedly an extra-social being. But simply to shut him out, as has been done up till now, means a repression of his growth, as though he were condemned to become dumb.

The solution of this conflict lies in preparing an environment adapted to these higher manifestations on the part of the child. When he says his first word there is no need to prepare anything and his baby language is heard in the house as a welcome sound. But the work of his small hands demands "motives of activity" in the form of suitable objects. We shall then see small children performing actions that demand an impressive effort, sometimes beyond what we should consider physically possible. I have here the photograph of a little English girl who is carrying a huge cottage loaf, so big that her arms cannot support the weight and she must rest it on her body. She has, therefore, to walk bending back so far that she cannot see where to put her feet. In the photograph we see only the anxiety of her dog, who will not let her out of his sight; he is all tense, as though about to bound to her help. But further off there were grown-up people, who had to make a great effort to keep themselves from running to take the loaf out of her arms.

Sometimes very tiny children show a precocious skill and accuracy of movement that must arouse our wonder. If an environment is prepared for them, they will take on complex social functions in their child world. I remember the deep impression made on me by a little boy of two who with great gravity waited on other children of the same age, preparing the table for them and doing the honours of the house. In these lofty labours he was plainly struck by two lighted candles which his mother had set on his birthday cake, for confusing the significance of things, he went about telling people, "I have two years and two candles."[1]

[1] "I Have two years"—literal translation of the Italian and French idiom for "I am two."

# 5

# Rhythm

## RHYTHM

The adult who has not grasped that manual activity is a vital need for the child, and who does not recognise the first manifestation of an instinct to work, prevents the child from working. This is not always the result of a defensive attitude, but may have other causes. One is that an adult looks at the outward purpose of an action, and has his own fixed mode of acting which is part of his mental make-up. To try to reach his ends by the most direct method, hence in the shortest possible time, has become for him a kind of natural law, which he has indeed formulated as "the law of least effort." Seeing the child make great efforts to perform a totally useless action, or one so futile that he himself could perform it in an instant and far better, he is tempted to help, as though to put an end to a disturbing spectacle. The enthusiasm he sees in a small child over such trivial things irritates him as something absurd and incomprehensible. If a child notices that a tablecloth is set askew on a table and remembers how it is usually spread, he will try to put it right in exactly the way he remembers, and, if he can do so, he does it slowly but with all the energy and enthusiasm of which he is capable; for to remember is his mind's chief task, and to put something to right as he has seen it, is the supreme triumph corresponding to his stage of development. But he is only able to do this when no grown-up is by to notice his effort.

If a child tries to brush his own hair the grown-up, instead of feeling overjoyed at this marvellous attempt, feels an assault on the very laws of his being. He sees that the child cannot brush his hair well, nor quickly, and will not attain the desired end, while he, the adult, can do it so quickly and so much better. Whereupon the child, who is delightedly performing one of those actions that build up his personality, sees the grown-up, a great big figure nearly as tall as the ceiling, immeasurably strong, and against whom there can be no resistance, coming up to him and taking the brush away, saying that he will do the brushing. A grown-up does the same if he sees a small child painfully trying to dress himself, or to do up his shoes. Every attempt made by the child is interrupted. The adult is irritated not only by the fact that the child is trying to perform an action when there is no need, but also by his different rhythm, his different manner of moving. Rhythm is not like an old idea that can be changed, or a new idea that can be understood. Each individual has a rhythm in his movements that is part of him, an intrinsic characteristic, almost like the shape of his body, and if this rhythm is in harmony with other similar rhythms, it cannot be adapted to different rhythms without suffering. If, for example, we are near a paralytic and must walk by his side, we feel an intense discomfort, and if we see a paralytic slowly raising a glass to his lips, at the risk of spilling its contents, the insufferable clash of different rhythms brings a discomfort from which we seek to free ourselves by substituting our own rhythm for that of the other; and this we call helping him. The adult with the child does something of the same kind. As if in unconscious defence he tries to prevent the child from making those slow clumsy movements, just as he would irresistibly brush away a harmless fly which annoyed him.

Contrariwise, the adult can endure the child's movements when they are swift, in a quicker rhythm, in this case he is ready to put up with the disorder and disturbance introduced into his environment by the child. Here the adult can "arm himself with patience," for here is something clear and manifest, and the adult's will can always control his conscious acts. But when there is a slowness in the child's movements, the adult is irresistibly impelled to *substitution*. Thus instead of helping the child in his most essential psychic needs, the adult substitutes himself for the child in all the acts the child wants to perform by himself, thus closing every path of activity to him and becoming the mightiest impediment to the development of his life. The despairing shrieks of the "naughty" child who does not want to be washed, or dressed, or have his hair brushed, are scenes in the earliest drama of human struggle.

Who would ever have thought that the *useless assistance* given to the child is the first root of all *repressions* and hence of the most perilous injury the adult individual can do to the child?

The Japanese mind has attained an impressive conception of the children's hell. As part of their cult of the dead they lay in the tombs of children a quantity of little stones or stone-like objects, to help them to save themselves from the torments that the demands of the other world will continually try to inflict on them. When the child is building something, a demon will knock it down and destroy it. And then the little stones provided by the pious care of his parents will enable him to rebuild it. Here is one of the most impressive projections of the subconscious into another life.

## ADULT SUBSTITUTION

The adult's substitution of his own action for that of the child does not only take the form of acting instead of him, but may show itself as an infiltration of the adult will into that of the child, so that it substitutes itself for the child's own will. Then it is no longer the child who acts, but the adult who acts through him.

When Charcot in his famous Institute of Psychiatry demonstrated the substitution of personality achieved by means of suggestion in the case of hysterical subjects, he made a sensation. His experiments undermined fundamental conceptions believed unshakable, namely that man is the master of his own actions. It was possible to prove experimentally that a suggestion could be imposed on a subject to such a point as to suppress his personality and substitute for it that of the hypnotist. These facts, though confined to the clinic and to a very restricted number of experiments, nonetheless opened a new field of research and discovery. Such phenomena led to studies on double personality, on subconscious and subliminal psychological states, and finally to exploration of the realm of the unconscious by psychoanalysis.

There is a period of life extraordinarily open to suggestion—the period of infancy—when consciousness is in process of formation and sensibility towards external factors is in a creative state. The adult can then insinuate his own personality, as though by subtle infiltration, into the child, so as to animate by his own will that sublime quality of the child's will, its fluidity.

We noticed in our schools that if in showing a child how to do anything we did so with too much enthusiasm, or performed the movements with too much energy or excessive accuracy, we quenched the child's capacity of judging and acting according to his own personality. The resxilt is, as it were, a movement detached from the ego that should command it, and taken from another extraneous and stronger ego which, by a slight motion, has the tremendous power of seizing, almost of stealing from the child's personality its own tender organs. It is not only wilfully that the adult exercises suggestion, but even without willing it or knowing it, and without having realised the existence of the problem.

I shall give a few examples. One day I myself saw a child of about two, who had put a pair of shoes on a white bed cover. With an unreflecting movement, impulsive, not measured, I took the shoes and put them on the ground in a corner saying "That's dirty!" and with my hand I brushed the cover where the shoes had lain. After this the child, whenever he saw a pair of shoes, ran to pick them up and put them in another place, saying "Dirty!" after which he would pass his hand over a bed as if to brush it, though the shoes had never been near it.

Another example. A family receives a parcel, which the mother greets with expressions of delight. She opens it and finds a piece of silk, which she immediately hands to her little girl, then a small trumpet, which she puts to her lips to play. The child cries joyfully, "Music!" For some time the little girl, whenever she touched a piece of cloth, grew rather excited and said, "Music!"

Inhibiting factors are especially liable to be infiltrated by an extraneous will into the acts of a child, when the will of the adult does not act sufficiently violently to provoke a reaction. This comes to pass particularly among well-behaved, self-controlled people, and especially through refined nurses. A most illuminating case I encountered was that of a child of about four, who was alone with her grandmother in her own home. The little girl showed a wish to turn on the tap of a fountain to see the gush of water, but just as she was about to do it, she drew back her hand. Her grandmother encouraged her to turn on the tap, but the child answered "No, Nurse doesn't allow it."

The grandmother tried to persuade her that she herself gave her full consent, pointing out to her that she was in her own home. The little girl smiled with pleasure, showing her contentment and above all her eagerness to see the fountain play, but, though she stretched out her arm to the tap, at the last moment her hand drew back without turning it. The sense of obedience to an order from the absent nurse was so powerful that the affectionate persuasions of someone near at hand could not outweigh that distant force.

A similar case was that of a bigger child, of about seven, who, when he was sitting down and wanted to get up and run to something in the distance that attracted him, had to come back and sit down, as though by an oscillation in his will which he could not overcome. No one knew who was the "master" who commanded within him, for of this the child's memory had lost all trace.

We may say that the openness of children to suggestion is an exaggeration of one of their constructive psychological functions, namely of a characteristic inner sensibility that we have called "love of the environment". The child observes things eagerly and is attracted by them, but above all he is attracted by the actions of the grown-up, and seeks to know and to reproduce them. Now in this the grown-up may have a kind of mission: that of inspiring the childish actions, of being an open book in which the child may read guidance for his own movements and learn what he should learn in order to act properly. But if this is to be the case, the adult must be always calm and act *slowly* so that all the details of his action may be clear to the child who is watching. If the adult abandons himself to his usual quick, powerful rhythms, then instead of inspiring he may engrave his own personality on the child's and substitute himself for the child by suggestion.

Even inanimate objects, if they are attractive to the senses, can have a power of suggestion in that they may force themselves upon the child's notice, like magnets attracting from without. To make this clear I will quote an interesting experiment made by Professor Levine and which he illustrates by his psychological films. He wished to note the different behaviour of defective and of normal children in our schools (taking care to choose children of about the same age and environment) when confronted by the same objects.

In this film we see a long table prepared, with a number of different objects on it, including some of our apparatus. A group of children comes in. They are at once attracted, interested by the objects before them. They are lively and full of smiles, and look pleased to find themselves among so many things. Each takes up something and sets to work, then puts it down and chooses another and so on, making one experiment after another. That is one picture.

Here is another. A second group of children conies in. They move slowly, stop, look round. They make for one of the many objects and stand round it for some time, and then they seem to stand still, inactive. That is the second picture.

Which of these two groups of children is that of the defectives and which that of the normal ones? The defectives are the lively, happy children, who move quickly, pass from one thing to another, and want to try everything. To the public it is they who seem the intelligent ones, for everyone is used to thinking that lively, gay children who flit from one thing to another are intelligent.

And instead the normal children are those that are seen moving calmly, spending much time in standing still and then fixing upon one thing as though in reflection. Hence calm, restrained and measured movement, and a thoughtful disposition are the attributes of normality.

The experiment reproduced by the two pictures seems to conflict with generally established ideas; for in an ordinary environment intelligent children act like the defective children of the film. The normal child, slow, reflective, is a new type, but he shows at once that his controlled movements are ruled by his ego and governed by reason. Such children master the suggestion that comes to them from outward things and deal with such things in freedom. The important thing is thus not a great deal of movement but self-mastery. The important thing for any individual is not that he should move anyhow and in any sense, but that he should have gained the mastery of his motor organs. The ability to move as directed by his own ego and not as dominated by the pure attraction of outward things, leads a child to concentrate on one thing only, and this is a phenomenon of inner origin.

Such delicate and thoughtful movement is the truly normal state; it sums up an order that we may call an order of inner discipline. Discipline in outward acts is the expression of an inner discipline that has crystallised round order. When this does not happen, movement passes out of the control of the personality and may be dominated by an extraneous will, and it will remain at the mercy of external objects, like a ship without a rudder. It is difficult for an extraneous will to produce disciplined activity because the organisation for such activity is wanting. And then we may say that the individuality is broken up. The child who has lost the opportunity of developing according to his own nature could almost be compared to a man who has landed from a balloon in a desert, and who all at once sees his balloon carried away by the wind. He will not be able to do anything to guide it and he sees nothing near him that will take its place. That is a picture of man as he really develops through the struggle between the adult and the child. His is a darkened mind, undeveloped and remote from his means of expression, which are as though left to the mercy of the elements.

## THE IMPORTANCE OF MOVEMENT

It is very clear that since the adult has had no notion of how important activity is to the child, he has simply prevented such disturbing activity.

It is not equally clear how scientists and teachers have failed to note the supreme importance of activity in the building up of the man-to-be. The very word "animal" implies the idea of animation, that is, of activity: the difference between animals and vegetables is that vegetables stand still and animals move. How then could it ever have been thought desirable to subdue the activities of a child?

Various expressions of praise show a subconscious acceptance of such an attitude. The child is called a "little flower"—something that keeps still. Or else, "a little angel," that is, a being that moves, nay, flies, but in another world from the world of men. ,

All this reveals the mysterious blindness of the human soul extending far beyond the narrow limits assigned by Freud to psychological *scotoma*, which he describes as a partial blindness existing in the unconscious of humanity.

This blindness is deep indeed if science, with its systematic methods for discovering the unknown, has passed by the most formidable testimony of human life without revealing it.

All have agreed on the importance of the senses in building up the mind. No one doubts that the mind of a deaf mute, or of a blind child, encounters extraordinary difficulties in its development, for sight and hearing are the gates of the mind; they are known as the intellectual senses. It is also agreed that intrinsic conditions being equal, the intelligence of deaf mutes and of the blind remains inferior to that of men who enjoy the use of all their senses. Yet the sufferings of the blind and deaf are plain to all, though they are other than physical sufferings, and even compatible with perfect health. No one would be so absurd as to suppose that by artificially depriving children of sight and hearing they would be made better able to assimilate intellectual culture and social morality. Nor could anyone ever think that for the progress of civilisation we must look to the deaf and blind.

But it would be hard to gain acceptance for the idea that movement has as much and more importance for the moral and intellectual building up of man. Man, if he builds himself, neglecting his organs of movement, will have an arrested development and remain permanently in a graver state of inferiority than that which arises from the absence of one of the intellectual senses.

The sufferings of the man who remains *the prisoner of his flesh* present a more tragic and significant picture than the sufferings of those deaf or blind. The blind and the deaf lack only the elements in their environment that act as external means to their development. The soul has such powers of adaptation that up to a certain point the keenness of one sense may supply the deficiency of another. But movement is a part of man's very personality, and nothing can take its place. The man who does not move is injured in his very being and is an outcast from life.

\* \* \*

When people speak of muscles they have at once the idea of a mechanism, indeed of the mechanism of a machine. And this seems very far removed from the idea we have formed of the spirit, which is remote from matter and mechanisms.

To attribute to movement even greater importance than to the so-called intellectual senses in the development of mind and in the intellectual evolution of a man, seems a defiance of accepted ideas.

But in the eye and ear there are mechanisms. Nothing could be more perfect than the sublime, living camera we find in the eye. And the ear

is an assembly of many-stringed harps with a jazz-band complete even
to the drum!

When, however, we speak of the importance of these sublime
instruments in building up the intelligence, we do not think of them
as mechanisms, but we think of the ego that uses them. Through these
marvellous vital instruments the ego comes into relation with the world
and uses them according to its psychological needs. The sight of the
beauties of nature, of sunrise or sunset, or of works of art, the sonorous
impressions of the outer world, man's voice, or music, all these manifold
and continuous impressions give the inner ego the delights of psychic
life and the nourishment necessary for its conservation.

The ego is the real agent, the single arbiter, and the recipient of the
sense impressions. If there were no ego to see and enjoy, what would be
the use of the mechanisms of the sensory organs? It is not the fact of
seeing or hearing that is important, but the fact that the ego should form
itself, grow, enjoy and maintain itself, through seeing and hearing.

Now we can draw an analogy between this and movement. Movement,
without any doubt, has its mechanical organs, though these are not
rigid and fixed like the membrane of the tympanum or the crystal lens
of the eye. Now the fundamental problem of human life and hence of
education is that the ego should be able to animate and master its own
instruments of motion, in order that in its actions it should be guided
by something higher than material objects or the functions of vegetative
life, something which is generally instinct, but which in man is openly
a creative spirit, clothed with intelligence.

If the ego cannot attain this essential condition its unity will be
shattered. It will be as though an instinct were to go about the world
separated from the body it should animate.

## "INTELLIGENCE OF LOVE"

The whole labour of life, which fulfils itself subject to its laws and brings
beings into harmony, reaches consciousness under the form of LOVE.

It is not the motor impulse, but it is a reflection of the motor impulse,
as planets reflect the light of the sun. The motor is instinct, the creative
urge of life. But this, in bringing creation to being, tends to make love

felt, and therefore love fills the consciousness of the child. His self-realisation comes about in him through love.

Indeed it is as love of his environment that we may envisage the irresistible urge which, throughout the sensitive periods, unites the child to things. It is not love in the sense that is commonly understood, as an emotional feeling, but a love of the intelligence which sees and assimilates and builds itself through loving. Yes, the inner guide that leads children to observe what is about them could be described, in Dante's phrase, as "intelligence of love."

It is indeed a form of love that gives them the faculty of observing in such an intense and meticulous manner the things in their environment that we, grown cold, pass by unseeing. Is it not a characteristic of love, that sensibility that enables a child to see what others do not see? That collects details that others do not perceive, and appreciates special qualities, which are, as it were, hidden, and which only love can discover? It is because the child's intelligence assimilates by loving, and not just indifferently, that he can see the invisible. This active, ardent, meticulous, constant absorption in love is characteristic of children.

To the adult, liveliness and joy are considered typical of the child's intensity of life; these are recognised as infant characteristics. There has been no recognition of the love behind them, that is to say, the spiritual energy, the moral beauty that accompanies creation.

The child's love is still pure of contrasts. He loves because he takes in, because nature orders him to do so. And what he takes he absorbs to make it a part of his own life, so as to create his own being.

In the child's environment the adult is a special object of love. From him the child receives material things and help, and from him the child takes, with intense love, what is necessary for his self-making. The adult is the venerable being from whose lips, as from a spiritual fountain, the words issue that will enable that child to build his own speech, and which will serve him as a guide. For the child, the words of a grown-up are supernatural stimuli. It is he, the grown-up, who by his action shows the child, who has come from nothing, how men move. To imitate him is to enter into life. The child is enchanted and fascinated by his words and actions, which even assume the force of suggestion: hence the child is sensitive to the grown-up to such a degree that his own personality may vanish and the grown-up live and work in him instead. The incident of the child who had put the dirty shoes on the bed-cover shows an obedience carried to the point of suggestion. What the grown-up tells him remains engraved in his mind, like words incised by a chisel on stone. The word "music", uttered by the mother who had received the parcel, is another instance. Therefore, the adult should count and measure all his words before the child; for the child is hungry to take from him; he is an accumulator of love.

The child is disposed to obey the adult, in the very roots of his spirit. Only when the adult asks him to deny the commands of the inner impulse urging him to creation by unalterable rules and laws, does it become impossible for the child to obey. It is then as if someone were to tell him, when he is teething, to stop and to let no more teeth appear. The fits of temper and disobediences of the child are the expression of a vital conflict between his creative urge and his love for the grown-up who does not understand him. When instead of obedience the grown-up encounters temper, he should always consider this conflict, and take into account the defence of a vital act necessary to the child's growth.

We must indeed realise that the child wants to obey us and loves us. The child loves the grown-up beyond anything, but people speak only of the grown-up's love for the child. This is said not only of parents but of teachers, "Teachers love children!" It is said also that the child must be taught to love, to love his mother, his father, his teacher, to love all men, to love animals, flowers, everything.

Who then will teach him? Who will be his master in the art of love? Those who put down all his spontaneous manifestations to naughtiness and who think of defending themselves and their possessions against him? It is clear that such cannot teach him to love; for they have no longer the sensitivity that we have called "intelligence of love."

It is, on the contrary, the child who loves the adult, who wants him near, to be always with him and whose delight lies in calling his attention to himself, "Look at me, stay with me."

When the child goes to bed in the evening he calls the loved person and begs him not to go away. When we go in to dinner the tiny child that still feeds at his mother's breast would like to come with us, to stay near to watch us, not to eat. The adult passes by this mystical love without perceiving it. But the little one who so loves us will grow up, will vanish. And who will ever love us as he does ? Who else will ever summon us on going to bed, saying, "Stay with me"? When the child is grown, he will say an indifferent "Good night". Who then will be eager just to watch us while we eat, though he eats nothing? We defend ourselves against this love that will pass away, and we shall never find anything to equal it. We in our turmoil say, "I haven't time, I can't, I have a lot to do," and we think in our hearts, "The child must be taught better, or he will make us his slaves." What we want is to be free from him to do what we ourselves like doing, so as not to give up our convenience.

It is terrible naughtiness in the child if he goes to wake up his father and mother of a morning, when they are still asleep. A nurse, where social conditions allow, must prevent this more than anything. A nurse is the guardian of the parents' morning sleep.

And yet, what is it but love that urges the child to go to his parents as soon as he wakes? And where he can, he gets out of bed early, like every other pure creature, when the sun appears. The child goes to find his parents who are still asleep, as if to say, "learn to live holily; it is light, it is morning." But he does not go to them as a teacher, he only runs to see those he loves. Perhaps the rooms are still dark, curtained so that the morning light shall not disturb the sleepers. Perhaps the child goes stumbling, his heart beating for fear of the darkness, but he overcomes everything, he comes softly and touches them. His father and mother scold him; "Didn't I tell you not to wake me up in the morning?"

"But I didn't wake you," says the child. "I only touched you, I only wanted to give you a kiss."

It is as though he said, "I didn't want to wake you physically, I only wanted to waken your spirit."

Indeed the child's love has a great significance where we are concerned. His father and mother sleep all their lives, they have a tendency to sleep over everything, and it is necessary that a new creature should stir them and sustain them with a fresh and living energy that they have long lost. It is necessary that a creature who lives differently should come to tell them every morning, "There is another life, that you have forgotten. Learn to live better."

To live better. To feel the touch of love.

Man would degenerate without the child to help him to renew himself. If the adult does not waken, little by little a hard crust will form round him, and render him insensible. This makes us think of the words of the Last Judgment, when Christ will say to the lost, to those who have not made use of the means of improvement they have encountered in life: "Depart from me, you cursed.... I was a stranger and you took me not in; naked and you covered me not; sick and in prison and you did not visit me."

The answer: "Lord, when did we see Thee hungry or thirsty or a stranger or naked or sick or in prison and did not minister to Thee?"

"Amen I say to you, as long as you did it not to one of these least, neither did you do it to Me."

In the vivid description of the Gospel, it would seem that we must help the Christ hidden in every poor man, in every prisoner, in every sufferer. But if we paraphrased the marvellous scene and applied it to the child, we should find that Christ goes to help all men in the form of the child.

"I loved you, I came to waken you in the morning, and you drove Me away."

"Lord, when did You ever come into our house in the morning to waken us? And when did we drive You away?"

"The child that was born of you, who came to summon you, was I. The child who begged you not to leave him, was I."

Foolish ones that we are! It was the Messiah! It was the Messiah coming to waken us and to teach us how to love. And we saw only a child's naughtiness and so we have lost our hearts.

# PART II

## NOW

# PART II

# The New Education

# 6

# The Task of the Educator

## DISCOVERY OF THE TRUE CHILD

We must face the startling fact that the child has a psychic life of which the delicate manifestations pass unperceived and of which the adult may inadvertently mar the pattern or hinder the development.

The adult's environment is not a life-giving environment for the child. Rather it is an accumulation of obstacles, leading him to a creation of defences, to deforming efforts at adaptation, or else leaving him the victim of suggestion. It is the outward aspect he thus presents that has been considered in the study of child psychology; it is from this that his characteristics have been defined, as a basis for education. Child psychology is thus something that must be *radically revised*. As we have seen behind every surprising response on the part of a child, lies an enigma to be deciphered; every form of naughtiness is the outward expression of some deep-seated cause, which cannot be interpreted as the superficial, defensive clash with an unsuitable environment, but as expressing a higher, essential characteristic seeking manifestation. It is as though a storm were hindering the child's soul from coming forth from its secret hiding place, to show itself in the outer world.

It is plain that all the incidents that mask the hidden soul in its continual endeavours to actualise its life, all the fits of temper, struggles, deviations, give no idea of a *personality*. They are merely *a sum of characteristics*.

But there must be a personality behind them if the child, the spiritual embryo, is following a constructive pattern in his psychic development. There is a hidden man, a hidden child, a buried living being, who must be *liberated*. Here is the first urgent task of education: liberation in this sense means knowledge, or indeed a discovery of the unknown.

If there is an essential difference between what psychoanalysis has discovered and this psychology of the unknown child, it consists primarily in this: that what lies secret in the subconsciousness of the adult is something repressed by the individual himself. The individual himself must be helped to disentangle the tangled skein formed by complex and resisting adaptations, by the symbols and camouflage organised during a lifetime. Whereas the secret of the child is barely hidden by his environment, it is on the environment that we must set to work to enable the child to manifest himself freely, the child is at a period of creation and expansion, and it is enough to open the door. Indeed that which he is creating, which from not-being is passing into existence, and from potentiality to actuality, at the moment when it comes forth from nothing, cannot be complicated, and where it is a question of an expansive energy there can be no difficulty in its manifestation. Thus by preparing an open environment, an environment suited to this moment of life, natural manifestation of the child's psyche and hence the revelation of his secret should come about spontaneously.

Without this first step, efforts at education can only go further and further into an inextricable maze.

*  *  *

Here is the aim of the truly new education; first of all to discover the child and effect his liberation. In this, we may say, lies the problem of existence: simply to exist. There will be a further chapter covering the whole period of a child's development to adult state, which deals with the problem of the help that must be offered him. In both these chapters, however, the environment is fundamental; it must facilitate the expansion of the being in process of development by a reduction of obstacles to a minimum, and must allow free scope for a child's energies, by offering the necessary means for the activities to which they give rise. Now the adult himself is part of the child's environment; the adult must adjust himself to the child's needs if he is not to be a hindrance to him and if he is not to substitute himself for the child in the activities essential to growth and development.

## SPIRITUAL PREPARATION

The educator must not imagine that he can prepare himself for his office merely by study, by becoming a man of culture. He must before all else cultivate in himself certain aptitudes of a moral order.

The crucial point of the whole question is the manner in which he considers the child, and this cannot depend on external factors as though it demanded merely a theoretical knowledge of child nature or of modes of teaching and correction.

Here what we wish to emphasize is the fact that the educator must prepare himself *inwardly*. He must examine himself methodically in order to discover certain definite defects that may become obstacles in his relation with the child. To discover defects that have become part and parcel of his consciousness requires help and instruction just as we need another to observe and tell us what lies at the back of our eye.

In this sense the educator needs to be "initiated" into his or her inner preparation. He is too preoccupied with bad tendencies in the child, how to correct his undesirable actions, or the danger to his soul left by the residues of original sin.

Instead he should begin by seeking out his own defects, and such tendencies in himself as are not good. First let him "remove the beam that is in his own eye, then shall he see more clearly to remove the mote" that is in the child's. This inner preparation is something general; it is not the same as the specific seeking for perfection as in the case of members of religious communities. It is not necessary to become "perfect", free from every weakness, in order to become an educator. Indeed it is possible for those continually concerned with the perfection of their inner life to remain unconscious of the defects that prevent them from understanding the child. That is why it is necessary to learn, to be guided, to be trained to become educators.

We have in ourselves tendencies that are not good and which flourish like weeds in a field. (Original sin.) These tendencies are many; they fall into seven groups, known of old as the Seven Deadly Sins.

All deadly sins tend to separate us from the child; for the child, compared to us, is not only purer but has mysterious qualities, which we adults as a rule cannot perceive, but in which we must believe with faith; for Jesus spoke of them so clearly and insistently that all the Evangelists recorded His words: "Unless ye be converted and become as little children, ye shall not enter into the Kingdom of Heaven."

That which the educator must seek is to be able to see the child as Jesus saw him. It is with this endeavour, thus defined and delimited, that we wish to deal. The true educator is the man who rids himself of the inner obstacles which make the child incomprehensible to him; he is not simply the man who is ever striving to become better. Our instruction to educators consists in showing them what inner dispositions they need to correct, just as a doctor might point out the particular and definite disease that is weakening or threatening a physical organ.

Here, then, is some *positive* help.

The deadly sin that arises within us and prevents us from understanding the child is Anger.

But since no deadly sin acts alone, but always in combination or company with another, so Anger summons and combines with a sin of more noble appearance and hence more diabolical, Pride.

The evil tendencies which we have classified as the Seven Deadly Sins, may be corrected in two ways. One is interior: the individual once he is clearly aware of his defects seeks of his own will, with every effort, to fight against them and rid himself of them, by the help of the grace of God.

The other is a social corrective and is found in the external environment. It can be defined as a resistance opposed by external forms to the outer manifestations of our evil tendencies, thus impeding their development.

This counteractive effort of external forms has much influence. It is, one might say, the chief reminder of the existence in ourselves of moral defect, and in many cases it is this external reminder that leads us to reflect upon ourselves and thence to work vigorously and earnestly for our inward purification.

Let us consider the Seven Deadly Sins. Our Pride is mitigated by other people's opinion of us; our Avarice by the circumstances in which we live; Anger by the reaction of the strong; Sloth by the necessity of working for a living; Lust by the customs of society; Greed by the limited possibilities of obtaining more than we need; Envy by the necessity of conserving an appearance of dignity. These external factors are a continual and very salutary warning.

The social check, in short, forms a good foundation for the support of our moral equilibrium.

We do not, however, feel the same purity when our actions are moulded by the resistance of society as when they are performed in obedience to God. On the contrary, while the necessity of a voluntary correction of recognised errors meets in our soul with docile acceptance, we adapt ourselves less easily to the humiliating situation of accepting the control of others. We even feel more humiliated by such enforced compliance than by the error itself. When it is necessary to hold ourselves in check, when we cannot do otherwise, an instinct prompts us to uphold our worldly dignity by making it appear that we chose the inevitable ourselves. The little deceit of saying "I don't like it" of something beyond our reach, is one of the commonest moral pretences.

We meet the resistance by a small fiction, but this means that we are offering battle, not entering upon a way of perfection.

The result is that, as in all warfare, organisation soon becomes plainly desirable; individual tendencies find refuge in collective tendencies.

Persons with the same defect are led instinctively to support each other; they seek strength through union. They build, as it were, fortifications against the hosts that oppose their capital vices.

No one for instance will dare to say that an equitable distribution of wealth would displease the rich because they are grasping and slothful. But it will be said that such a distribution of wealth is beneficial to all and is a necessity of social progress, and then we shall find even many rich men declaring that they are resigned to it for the common good. We have an instinctive tendency to mask our sins by protestations of lofty and necessary duties, just as in the war a strip of ground dug with trenches or filled with death-dealing devices is camouflaged as a flowery meadow.

The weaker the external forces that oppose our defects the more time and ease we have to build the screens to camouflage our defences.

By pausing on these reflections, we come to realise that we are more attached to our vices than we think; we come to see how easy it is for the devil to creep in, teaching us to hide subconsciously even from ourselves.

In this we are defending, not our life, but our deadly sins. It is a mask we are only too ready to put on, calling it "necessity", "duty", "the common good", and so on, and from all this we find it daily harder to free ourselves.

Now the educator, or in general anyone, wishing to educate children must purge himself of that state of error that puts him in a position of falsity *towards the child*. The prevalent defect must be clearly defined; and here we are speaking not of one sin, but of a compost of two mortal sins closely allied—pride and anger.

Anger is truly the essential sin; pride follows to lend it a pleasing camouflage. Pride cloaks the personality of the grown-up in a series of robes which make it look pleasing and even entitled to respect.

Now anger is one of those sins that are held most easily in check by the strong and determined resistance of others. Anger is a manifestation which a man finds it hard to accept from others. Hence it is kept prisoner when confronted by strength. The man who speedily finds himself in the humiliating position of being forced to retreat becomes ashamed of his anger.

We therefore find a real outlet in meeting persons unable to defend themselves or to understand us, such as children who believe everything they are told. Children not only soon forget our offences, but feel guilty of all of which we accuse them. They are like the holy disciple of St. Francis, who burst into tears thinking himself a hypocrite, because a priest told him so.

We would have the educator here reflect upon the very serious effects of such conditions on the child's life. It is only the child's reason that fails to realise the injustice; his spirit feels it and becomes oppressed or even deformed. Childish reactions then appear, as expressions of an unconscious defence. Timidity, lying, caprice, frequent tears without apparent cause, sleeplessness, every form of exaggerated fear—obscure things like these represent unconscious defensive states in the little child, whose intelligence is not yet able to grasp his real relation to the grown-up.

But anger does not always mean physical violence.

The crude, primitive impulse usually understood by this word may lead to complex manifestations. The man of greater psychological maturity masks and complicates his inner states of sin.

In fact, anger in its simple form comes out only as a reaction to open resistance by the child. But in the presence of more obscure expressions of the child soul, anger and pride fuse together in a complex whole which assumes that precise, quiet, and respectable shape, known as *tyranny.*

Here we have an oppression that is not disputed, placing the tyrannous individual in an impregnable fortress of recognised authority. The adult is in the right simply because he is adult. To question this would be like attacking an established and sacred form of sovereignty. The tyrant in primitive societies used to be considered a delegate of God. But, for the child, the grown-up is God Himself. The thing is beyond dispute. Indeed, the only being who could dispute it would be the child, and he must remain silent. He must adapt himself to everything, he believes everything, forgives everything. When cuffed, he does not retaliate, and he willingly asks the angry grown-up to pardon him, forgetting even to ask wherein he has offended.

Yet the child does occasionally act in self-defence, but his defence is hardly ever a direct and intentional reply to the action of the adult. It is either a vital defence of his psychic integrity, or else an unconscious reaction of the oppressed spirit.

Only as the child grows older does he begin to direct his reaction against the tyranny itself; but, then, the adult finds justificatory reasons wherewith to entrench himself still more firmly behind his camouflage, and succeeds sometimes in convincing even the child that such tyranny is for his good.

"Respect" is on one side only; the weak respecting the strong.

It is thought legitimate for the adult to "offend" the child. He can judge the child, or speak ill of him, and does it openly, even so as to hurt his feelings.

The child's needs are directed or suppressed by the adult at will. A protest from the child is considered insubordination that it would be dangerous to tolerate.

This is a form of government on a primitive model, when the subjects have only to pay their taxes without question. There have been people who believed that every good was secured to them by the beneficence of their sovereign, and in the same way children think that they owe all to the adult. Or rather, it is the adult who instilled this belief. His camouflage of creator is organised. He in his pride believes that he creates in the child all that he is. It is the adult who makes the child intelligent, good, and religious; that is, provides him with the means he will need for communication with his environment, with men, and with God. This is a difficult task. To complete the picture the adult denies that he is a tyrant. Where is the tyrant who ever confessed to sacrificing his subjects?

The preparation our method demands of the educator is that he should examine himself, and purge himself of his sins of tyranny, he must tear down that ancient complex of pride and anger that unconsciously encrusts his heart; strip himself of pride and anger and become humble, this first of all; then re-clothe himself in charity. These are the spiritual qualities he has to acquire. This is the central point of balance without which it is impossible to proceed. This is his "training", its starting point, and its goal.

We do not mean that he must approve all the child's acts or refrain from judging him, or that nothing has to be done to help the development of his intelligence or feelings. Quite the contrary; it must not he forgotten that the aim is to educate, to become a real helper to the child.

But first comes an act of humility, the rooting-out of a prejudice embedded in our hearts; just as the priest before going up to the altar must recite his *Confiteor*.

So, and not otherwise.

We do not hold that the child should be denied such help as education can give him, but that there must be a radical change in our own inner state, which prevents us as adults from understanding him.

# 7

# Our Own Method

## HOW IT ORIGINATED

Our own method of education is characterised by the central importance that we attribute to the question of environment. Another innovation that has aroused much interest and controversy has been the role of the educator—the passive educator—who holds his own activities and authority in abeyance, lest they should be an obstacle preventing the child from acting for himself, and who is glad when he sees the child so acting, making progress on his own, and seeks no credit for it. He applies to himself the words of St. John the Baptist: "He must increase: but I must decrease." Another characteristic principle is respect for the child's personality, carried to a degree unattained in any other educational method.

These three essential points were developed in special educational institutions, which were called in the beginning *Casa dei Bambini*, literally children's houses, and suggest a familiar environment. Those who have followed this educational movement know that it has always aroused much discussion, especially in view of the reversed roles of adult and child: the educator who does so little actual teaching, with the child the centre of activity, learning by himself, left free in his choice of occupation and in his movements. This, when it was not considered an utopia, was held to be an exaggeration. Whereas our conception of a material environment in which everything should be in proportion to the size of a child, has been well received. The clear, lighted rooms, with little low windows, wreathed in flowers, with small pieces of furniture of every shape just like the furniture of a nicely furnished home, little tables, little armchairs, pretty curtains, low cupboards within reach of the children's hands, where they can put things and from which they can take what they want, all this seemed a real, practical improvement in a child's life. I believe that the greater number of *Casa del Bambini* maintain this external criterion as of prime importance.

To-day, after long research and experience, we feel a need to return to the question and especially to explain how our method originated.

It would be a great mistake to believe that by casually observing children we were led to frame such a bold idea as that of the existence of a hidden nature in the child, and that such an intuition in its turn gave rise to the idea of a special school and a special method of education. It is impossible to observe something that is not known, and it is not possible for anyone all at once, by a vague intuition, to imagine that a child may have two natures and to say, "Now I will try to prove it by experiment." Anything new must emerge so to speak, by its own energies; it must spring forth and strike the mind, evoked by what we call chance. Often there is no one more incredulous than the person to whom this happens; he rejects the new fact just like everyone else. The novelty must present itself again and again before it is finally seen, recognised and eagerly received. Then indeed the eagerness with which he who perceives it welcomes the new light, cherishes it, enthuses over it and dedicates his life to it, may make others believe that it was his creation. Whereas he has merely reached a point where he could recognise it, and has done like the man in the Bible, who, when he had found one pearl of great price, went his way and sold all that he had and bought it. Our difficulty lies in perceiving, in convincing ourselves of something new, for the gates of our apprehension are closed against novelty. Our mind is like an aristocratic drawing-room, which is closed to people without credentials; to gain admittance it is necessary to be introduced by someone already known—we proceed from the known to the unknown. Whereas what is *new* must break down the closed doors, or else creep in at a moment of relaxation when the door has been left ajar. Then the novelty produces amazement, revolution. Volta must have gazed incredulously at the twitching legs of the dead, skinned frog. None the less he noted the fact, and isolated electricity. Sometimes the most trivial fact may open illimitable horizons, for man is by nature a seeker, an explorer; but without the discovery of the initial trivial facts, no advance is possible.

In physics and medicine we have rigorous ideas as to what constitutes a new phenomenon. A new phenomenon is an initial discovery of facts, previously unknown and therefore unsuspected, that is to say, that were as if they did not exist. A fact is always objective and therefore cannot depend on an intuition. When it is a case of proving the existence of a new fact, it must be proved that it exists of itself, that is, it must be isolated. Then comes a second phase, the study of the conditions in which the new phenomenon shows itself, so that we may reproduce it and thus perpetuate it. Only when this fundamental problem has been solved, is it possible to study the phenomenon; it is then that research begins, and, finding new things on the new path, investigators may make further genuine discoveries. This is another matter; it is clear that no one can search for something he does not know exists. Research must have an ante-chamber; it implies an apparition. There is a form of studies exclusively concerned with reproducing, maintaining and gaining mastery over a phenomenon, so that it shall not vanish like a vision, but become a reality, a manageable possession, and hence a real value.

Now the first *Casa dei Bambini* was not a place arranged for a determined educational experiment, or for scientific educational research. It provides an example of an initial discovery which had all the features of an "unknown" presenting itself before it had been recognised, of a trivial fact able to open illimitable horizons.

Something I wrote long ago, which I have discovered in a heap of old papers, may be of documentary interest in this respect.

## "WHO ARE YOU?"

"It was January 6th (1907), when the first school was opened for small, normal children between three and six years of age. I cannot say on my methods, for these did not yet exist. But in the school that was opened my method was shortly to come into being. On that day there was nothing to be seen but about fifty wretchedly poor children, rough and shy in manner, many of them crying, almost all the children of illiterate parents, who had been entrusted to my care.

"The initial plan was to gather the small children of the workmen living in a workers' tenement, so that they should not be left to play on the stairs and dirty the walls or create disorder. With this end in view a room, a shelter or asylum, had been provided for them in the tenement. I had been asked to take charge of this institution, which 'might have a future'.

"I had a strange feeling that made me announce emphatically at the opening that here was a 'grandiose' undertaking of which the whole world would one day speak.

"The words of Scripture which on that day, the Epiphany, were read in the churches, seemed to me an omen and a prophecy: 'For behold darkness shall cover the earth... but the Lord shall arise upon thee, and the Gentiles shall walk in thy light'. All present were stupefied, and asked each other why on earth I should attribute so much importance to an institution for poor children.

"I set to work feeling like a peasant woman who, having set aside a good store of seed-corn, has found a fertile field in which she may freely sow it. But I was wrong. I had hardly turned over the clods of my field, when I found gold instead of wheat; the clods concealed a precious treasure. I was not the peasant I had thought myself. Rather I was like Aladdin, who, without knowing it, had in his hand a key that would open hidden treasures.

"In fact, my work on these normal children brought me a series of surprises. Possibly this marvellous fairy-tale is worth telling.

"It was logical to think that those methods which had met with much success in the training of defectives might prove a real key to the better development of normal children, and that those means by which I had had remedial success in strengthening weak minds and straightening deviated intelligences, held the principles of a hygiene of the mind, excellent for assisting normal minds to grow strong and straight.[1] In all this there was nothing wonderful, and the educational theory which has resulted

---

[1] Cf. Dr. Maria Montessori: *The Discovery of the Child*, Chapter II (published by Kalakshetra, Madras 20).

is as positive and scientific as it could be made, to convince balanced and prudent minds. But this does not obviate the fact that the first, unexpected results found me amazed and often incredulous.

"The objects presented to the normal children did not have the same effect on them as on defectives. With the backward children the apparatus had been useful to *me* as a means of arousing their interest, and I had to put forth all my energy to persuade the children to work with them; then indeed the apparatus enabled the defective children to improve in mental health and to learn something. But here the exact opposite occurred. The child was attracted by the object, fixed his attention on it, and went on working and working without rest, in a wonderful state of concentration. After such work, he *then* seemed satisfied, rested and happy. Yes, it was restfulness that you could read on those serene little faces, in the childish eyes that shone with contentment after the performance of a spontaneous task. It was as if the objects in question were like the key that winds a clock. After a moment's winding, the clock goes of itself. But here the child after working was stronger and mentally healthier than before. Such work was a real mental tonic.

"It took time for me to convince myself that this was not an illusion. After each new experience proving such a truth, I said to myself, 'I won't believe yet, I'll believe it next time'. Thus for a long time I remained incredulous, and at the same time deeply stirred and anxious. How many times did I not reprove the children's teacher when she told me what the children had done of themselves? 'The only thing that impresses me is truth,' I would reply severely. And I remember that the teacher answered, without taking offence, and often moved to tears: 'You are right. When I see such things I think it must be the holy angels who are inspiring these children.'

"One day, in great emotion, I took my heart in my two hands as though to encourage it to rise to the heights of faith, and I stood respectfully before the children, saying to myself: 'Who are you then? Have I perhaps met with the children who were held in Christ's arms and to whom divine words were spoken?... I will follow you, to enter with you into the Kingdom of Heaven.'

"And holding in my hand the torch of faith, I went on my way."

### THE FIRST CHILDREN

It was thus that chance led me to them. They were tearful, frightened children, so shy that it was impossible to get them to speak; their faces were expressionless, with bewildered eyes as though they had never seen anything in their lives. They were indeed poor, abandoned children, who had grown up in dark, tumble-down slum-dwellings, with nothing to stimulate their minds, and without care. Everyone could see they suffered from malnutrition; it was not necessary to be a doctor to recognise that they were in urgent need of food, open air life and sunlight. They were closed flowers, but without the freshness of buds, souls concealed beneath a hermetic shell.

It would be interesting to know the original circumstances that enabled these children to undergo such an extraordinary transformation, or rather, that brought about the appearance of new children, whose souls revealed themselves with such radiance as to spread a light through the whole world.

These circumstances must have been singularly favourable to enable the "liberation of the soul of the child". All repressive obstacles must have been eliminated. But who could have told in what such obstacles consisted? And what were the favourable, or indeed necessary circumstances, that enabled a buried soul to come forth and flower? Many would have seemed the exact opposite to what was required for such a lofty goal.

Let us begin with the family circumstances of these children. They came from the lowest strata of society; for their fathers were not workmen in regular employment, but casual workers who sought for temporary work from day to day, and who therefore could not look after their children. Nearly all were illiterate.

Since it was not possible to find a proper mistress for a post that offered no future prospects, the first idea was that the porter's daughter should be employed more or less as a guardian; later a better educated girl was engaged, who, though she had once started to study to be a teacher, at that time worked as a factory hand and hence had no ambitions as mistress and none of the preparation—or prejudice—that would have been inevitable in any real teacher. The new institution was in a peculiar position in that it was not a true charitable organisation, but founded by a building society, which counted the cost of the school as an indirect item in the upkeep of the building. The children were collected there so that the walls should remain intact and the tenement have less frequent need of renovation. We could not, therefore, undertake welfare work such as the provision of school meals, medical treatment or a real school with an educational aim. The only expenditure allowed for was what would have been required by any office; furniture and supplementary equipment. It was because of this that we had to have our furniture made, instead of buying desks.

If conditions had not been so peculiar, it would not have been possible to isolate the purely psychological factors or to prove their influence on the transformation of these children.

The *Casa dei Bambini* was thus not a real school, but like a measuring meter, which at the beginning of an undertaking, is set at zero.

Thus, it was impossible to obtain desks for the children, or a teacher's desk, or the usual equipment for a school, and special furniture was made, such as might be made for an office or a house. At the same time I had some precise scientific apparatus prepared, such as I had already used in an institution for defectives, and which, therefore, had nothing about it that could cause it to be considered school equipment.

It must not be thought that the "environment" in the first *Casa dei Bambini* was gay and pretty like that associated with such institutions of today. The most impressive pieces of furniture were a stout table for the teacher, and a huge, massive cupboard in which to house all sorts of objects, and of which the thick doors were shut with keys that remained in the teacher's keeping. The tables intended for the children were made with a view to strength and durability; they were so long that three children sat in a row, and they were set one behind the other like the desks of a school. The only novelty was the provision of little seats and very simple little armchairs, one for each child. Even the flowers were lacking, that were later to become a characteristic feature of our schools, for the courtyard, though cultivated, contained only little lawns and trees. In such surroundings, there could be small inducement to undertake any important experiments, but I thought it would be interesting to attempt a systematic education of the senses, to test the possible differences of reaction between normal and defective children, and above all to find what promised to be an interesting correspondence between the reactions of younger normal children and those of older defective ones. I did not, however, set excessive store by such research. I laid no restrictions on the mistress, and I gave her no special duties, I merely taught her how to use some of the sensory apparatus, so that she could present them accurately to the children. This seemed to her easy and interesting. But I did not prevent her following her own initiative.

Indeed, after a little while I found that she herself had made further material—crosses, covered in gilt paper, which according to her would serve as rewards for the best behaved children. I often saw one or other of them wearing one of these harmless decorations on his breast. She had also taken upon herself to teach them all to make a military salute, though most of the children were little girls and the eldest was only five. But this seemed to give her satisfaction, and I found the whole thing as unimportant as it was silly.

Thus our life of peace and isolation started, and for a long time no one knew of our existence.

## WHAT THEY SHOWED ME

I should like to summarise just the principal events of this period, though to do so is to speak of such infinitesimal things that they would belong better to those children's stories that begin "Once upon a time..." than to a solemn treatise. My own actions in the matter were so simple, so truly puerile, that no one would wish to take them seriously from a scientific point of view. None the less a methodical description would mean a volume of psychological observations, or better, of discoveries.

### Repetition of the Exercise

The first phenomenon that awoke my attention was that of a little girl of about three who was practising slipping our series of solid cylinders in and out of the block (they go in and out of the holes like the corks of bottles, but they are cylinders of graduated size and each one has its own special place). I was surprised to see so small a child repeating an exercise over and over again with the keenest interest. She showed no progress in speed or skill; it was a kind of perpetual motion. My habit of measuring things led me to begin to count the number of times she repeated the exercise. Then I thought I would see how far the strange concentration she showed could withstand disturbance, and I told the teacher to make the other children sing and move about. They did so, but the little girl did not stop her work for an instant. Then I gently picked up the armchair in which she sat, with her in it, and put it on a little table. She had quickly clutched her cylinders to her, and, putting them on her knees, continued her work. From the time when I had begun to count, she had repeated the exercise forty-two times. She stopped, as though coming out of a dream, and smiled as if she were very happy. Her eyes shone, and she looked about her.

It seemed that she had not even noticed our various manoeuvres, which had not succeeded in disturbing her. And now, for no visible reason, her task was finished. What was finished, and why?

Here was a first peep into the unexplored depths of the child mind. Here was a very small child, at an age when attention flits from one thing to another and cannot be held down. Yet she had been absorbed in concentration such that her ego had withdrawn itself from reach of any external stimulus. That concentration was accompanied by a rhythmic movement of the hands, evoked by an accurately made, scientifically graduated object.

Similar facts occurred on various occasions. And every time the children emerged as if rested, full of life, with the look of those who have experienced some great joy.

Though such instances of a concentration reaching insensibility to the outer world were not usual, I noticed a peculiar behaviour that was common to all, and practically the rule in all they did—the special characteristic of child work, which I later called "repetition of the exercise".

Watching those dirty little hands at work I thought one day that I would teach the children something really useful, how to wash their hands. I noticed that the children, once their hands were clean, went on washing them. They came out of school and went to wash their hands. Some of the mothers told me that in the morning their children had run out of the house, and had been found at the washing tanks, washing their hands. They were proud to show everyone their clean hands, so much so that they were once mistaken for beggars. They repeated the performance again and again without having any longer an external aim in doing so. It was by an inner need that they went on washing hands that were already clean. The same thing happened on many other occasions; the more accurately an exercise was taught in all its details, the more it seemed to become a stimulus to an endless repetition of the same exercise.

## Their Feeling for Order

Another detail came to light for the first time as a result of a very simple incident. The children used the apparatus made for them, but it was the teacher who distributed it and put it back in its place. She told me that when she was doing this the children got up and came to stand around her. She sent them to their seats, but they always came back. This happened many times, and she had concluded that they were being disobedient. When I watched them, I understood that what they wanted was themselves to put the various objects back, and I left them to do so. Thus, a kind of new life began for them; to put things tidy, to tidy up any disorder that might have arisen, became an enthralling occupation. If a glass of water fell from a child's hands, others ran to pick up the pieces and dry the floor. One day the teacher dropped a box containing sixty-three tablets of various graduated colours. I remember her confusion, for it was difficult to recognise so many shades of colour, so as to know where each belonged. But at once the children ran to her, and to our amazement quickly put all the tablets in their places, correctly graduated, showing a wonderful sensibility to the colours, such as we did not possess.

## Free Choice

One day the teacher came to school a little late. She had forgotten to lock the cupboard, and she found that many children had opened the door and were standing round it. Some were taking things from it and carrying them away. The teacher decided that this revealed a thieving instinct. Children who stole and showed a lack of respect for their school and their teacher must, she said, be treated with severity and would have to be taught the difference between right and wrong. I, on the contrary, felt I should interpret the incident as implying that the children now knew the various objects and were able to choose among them. This, in fact, was the case. A lively and interesting form of activity now began. The children had their special preferences and chose their own occupations. To enable them to do so, we later provided low, pretty cupboards, in which the apparatus was placed at the disposition of the children, who could choose what corresponded to their inner needs. Thus the *Principle of free choice* accompanied that of *Repetition of the exercise.*

From this freedom of choice observations could be made with regard to the tendencies and psychical needs of the children.

One of the first interesting consequences seen was that the children did not choose all the scientific material prepared but only some of it. They used to choose more or less the same objects; some among them with evident preference. Other objects, instead, were left alone and slowly gathered dust.

I presented all of them and also made the teacher explain and demonstrate their use. Yet the children would not take them on their own.

I, then, understood that in the environment prepared for children everything should not only be kept in order, but also within certain measured limits and that interest and concentration arise where confusion and superfluity are eliminated.

## They Never Chose the Toys

Though the school contained some really wonderful toys, the children never chose them. This surprised me so much that I myself intervened, to show them how to use such toys, teaching them how to handle the doll's crockery, lighting the fire in the tiny doll's kitchen, setting a pretty doll beside it. The children showed interest for a time, but then went away, and they never made such toys the objects of their spontaneous choice. And so I understood that in a child's life play is perhaps something inferior, to which he has recourse for want of something better, but that there were loftier things which, in the child's mind, seemed to take precedence over useless amusements. The same might be said of ourselves; to play chess or bridge is pleasant enough for our leisure moments, but it would no longer be so if we were forced to do nothing else all through our life. When there is a lofty and urgent task to be done, bridge is forgotten, and the child has always lofty, and indeed urgent, tasks before him. Every passing minute is precious to him, representing the passage from a slightly inferior state of being to a higher one. The child is continually growing, and all that has to do with the means of his development fascinates him and makes him forget idle occupations.

## Rewards and Punishments

One day on coming into the school I saw a child sitting in a little armchair in the middle of the room, all by himself, doing nothing; on his chest he wore the pompous decoration that the teacher had prepared as a reward of good behaviour. The teacher told me that this child was being punished. But a moment earlier she had rewarded another child, pinning the decoration on him. And this child, passing beside the culprit, had passed the decoration on to him, as though it were something useless and in the way of anyone who wanted to work. The culprit looked at the decoration with indifference and then looked tranquilly about him, evidently without feeling his punishment. This was enough to show the vanity of rewards and punishments, but we wished to observe the children for a longer period, and after a vast number of experiments we found the fact so constantly repeated that the teacher ended by feeling almost ashamed both of rewarding and of punishing those children who set no store by either reward or punishment. After that we abolished rewards and punishments. What surprised us most was the frequency with which the reward was refused. The fact of the child who gave his decoration to the culprit, not as a reprisal but as the best thing to do with it, put the matter in a nutshell. But even before, we had so often seen those gilt crosses pinned to the breasts of children without arousing the smallest reaction; here then was an awakening of consciousness, the emergence of a delicate sense of dignity which formerly did not exist.

## Silence Exercise

One day I came into class holding in my arms a baby four months old, which I had taken from the arms of its mother in the courtyard. The little one was all enwound in swaddling-clothes, according to the custom of the people; its face was fat and pink, and it did not cry. The *silence* of the little creature struck me, and I wanted the children to share my feeling. "See," I said, "it isn't making a sound." And, joking, I added, "Look how still it keeps…. None of you could keep as still as that."

To my amazement I saw an extraordinary tension in the children who watched me. It seemed as though they were hanging on my lips, and felt deeply all I was saying. "Then its breathing," I went on, "how soft it is. None of you could breathe as it does, without making a sound...." The children, surprised and motionless, held their breath. In that moment there was an extraordinary silence; the tick of the clock, which generally could not be heard, became perceptible. It seemed as if the baby had brought with it an atmosphere of silence such as does not exist in ordinary life. This was because no one was making the smallest movement. And from this came the wish to listen to the silence, and hence to reproduce it. The children all sought to do so eagerly, if eagerness did not imply an impulsiveness that must find outward expression. Here instead was the expression of a correspondence born of deep-seated desire. At once the children sat still, controlling even their breathing, and so they remained, with the serene, intense look of those engaged in meditation. Little by little in that impressive silence little noises were heard, a drop of water falling in the distance, the far-off twitter of a bird. This incident was the origin of our silence exercise.

One day I had the idea of using silence to test the children's keenness of hearing, so I thought of calling them by name, in a low whisper, from a certain distance, as is the custom in certain medical tests. The child called was to come up to me, walking so as not to make a sound. With forty children this exercise in patient waiting demanded a patience that I thought impossible, so I brought with me some sweets as a reward for each child who came to me. *But the children refused the sweets.* They seemed to say, "Don't spoil our lovely experience, we are still filled with delight of the spirit, don't distract us." And so I realised that children were sensible not only to silence but to a voice calling imperceptibly in silence. They came up slowly, walking on tip-toe, taking care not to knock into things, and their footsteps could not be heard. Later it became clear to me that every exercise in movement that is susceptible of control by error, as in this case by noises in a silence, helps to guide children to perfect their powers; and thus the repetition of the exercise may lead to an external training in action, so delicate that it would be impossible to obtain it by external teaching. Our children learned to move among things without knocking into them, to run lightly without making a noise, and so became alert and agile. And they rejoiced in *the perfection of their achievements.* What interested them was to discover themselves, their capacities, and to *gain practice* in a mysterious world like that of evolving life.

## They Refused Sweets

It needed a long time for us to convince ourselves that the children's refusal of sweets had its intrinsic reason—sweets, given as prizes or for no reason, represented unnecessary and irregular food. This seemed to me so extraordinary that I wished to repeat the test again and again, for everyone knows that children are always greedy for sweets. I took sweets to school, but the children refused them or put them in the pockets of their aprons. Thinking that since they were poor they wanted to take the sweets home to their families, I told them, "These sweets are for you, and here are others for you to take home." They took them, but they put them all in their pockets, and did not eat them. Yet they appreciated them as gifts, for once, when one of these children was ill in bed and the mistress came to see him, he was so grateful that he opened a little box and took out a big sweet which had been given him at school, and offered it to her. That sweet had remained by him to tempt him for weeks, but he had not touched it. Was it a feeling like that of the monks who flee from ease and from such outward things as are useless to the true good of life, once they have risen on the ladder of spiritual life? It is certain that this phenomenon was so general among the children that in later schools not a few visitors came on purpose to verify it, and wrote about it in many books. Here was a spontaneous and natural psychological fact. Of course, no one thought of teaching penance and abolishing sweets, no one could have had such an extraordinary and fantastic idea as to assert: "Children should not play or eat sweets." When fantasy gets to work it does not do so on things of this kind. Curious anecdotes were told in the matter, like that which went round the world, about an important personage who distributed biscuits which happened to be of geometrical shapes, and how the children, instead of eating them, looked at them with interest, saying: "That's a circle! That's a rectangle!" There is another pretty story of a little child of poor parents who was watching his mother cooking. She picked up an intact piece of butter and the child said: "It's a rectangle." She cut off a corner and he said, "Now you've taken

a triangle," adding, "And it leaves a trapezium." And he never uttered
the usual plea: "Give me some bread and butter."

## Their Sense of Dignity

I can tell of other incidents that pointed to interesting characteristics.
One day I thought of giving a rather humorous lesson on how you blow
your nose. After having imitated various ways of using a handkerchief
for this purpose, I ended by showing how it can be done discreetly, so
as to make as little noise as possible, slipping out the handkerchief so
that the action remains more or less hidden. The children listened and
watched with the keenest attention, and did not laugh, and I wondered
to myself what could be the reason. But hardly had I finished than
there came a burst of applause, like when in the theatre a great actress
evokes an ovation repressed with difficulty. Then indeed I was utterly
amazed. I had never heard it said that such small children could turn
into an applauding audience, or that small hands could express themselves
with so much vigour. It occurred to me that perhaps I had touched
on a sensitive spot in the social life of this little world. The question
I had treated was one that children associate with a kind of continual
humiliation, a permanent derision; they are always being scolded about
blowing their noses. Everyone shouts at them, everyone insults them
(they are even habitually referred to as "snot-nose" among the people),
and in the end, especially in schools, handkerchiefs are pinned visibly to
their overalls, so that they shall not lose them. The handkerchief then
is like a stigma and badge of infamy. Yet, no one had ever taught them
without attacking them directly how they ought to blow their noses. We
should put ourselves in their place, or better, we should understand that
children are sensitive to all the derision that is showered upon them, and
which leaves them with a sense of humiliation. Such a lesson as mine did
them justice, redeemed them, enabled them to raise themselves in social
life. That was how I had to interpret it; for afterwards, through long
experience, I discovered that children have a profound feeling of personal
dignity and their souls may remain wounded, ulcerated, oppressed, in a
way the adult can never have imagined.

That day did not end so. When I was going away the children began
to shout "Thank you! Thank you for the lesson." And when I went out

they came behind me into the street, in a silent procession along the pavement, till I told them: "When you go back, run on tip-toe and take care not to knock into the corner of the wall." They turned round and disappeared through the gates as though on wings. I had indeed touched these poor little children in their social dignity.

One day an important visit was announced from someone who wished to remain alone with the children to observe them. I urged the teacher: "For this occasion, let everything happen spontaneously." And turning to the children, I told them: "Tomorrow you will have a visitor. How I would like him to think, 'these children are the best in the world'."

Later, I asked how the visit had gone off. "It was a great success," the teacher told me. "The children prepared a chair and said to the visitor, 'Won't you sit down?' And others said, 'Good morning.' Then when he went away, all crowded to look out of the window, shouting 'Thank you for your visit, good-bye'."

"But why all these compliments and preparations?" I asked. "I told you to do nothing out of the usual, and to let everything happen naturally."

"But I didn't say a word to them," she replied. "It was they themselves...." And she added, "Even I couldn't believe my eyes, and I said to myself that it must be the angels inspiring them...." She went on to tell me that the children had done their work well, each taking a different task, and going on with it so quietly that the visitor was really moved.

For a long time I remained doubtful and incredulous, tormenting the teacher to make sure that there were no preparations or rehearsals. But at last I understood. The children had their own sense of dignity, their *amour-propre,* and they knew how to organise their work and how to receive visitors with gratitude and cordial pleasure. They paid honour to their visitors, they were proud to show the best they could do. Had I not said to them, "I should like it to be thought that these children are the best in the world?" But it was certainly not through my exhortation that they acted as they did. It was enough to say, "You are to have a visitor," just as one announces a visitor in a drawing-room, and there was that little world alert and responsible, full of dignity and courtesy, to do the rest.

I understood then something very simple and yet almost extraordinary. *The children had no shyness.* No obstacles had been set between their souls and their surroundings, they had expanded fully and naturally, like lotus flowers opening their white petals to the full to the rays of the sun, and sending forth a delicate fragrance. They had nothing to hide, nothing to shut away, nothing to fear. That was all. Their ease was the result, we may say, of an immediate and perfect adaptation to their environment. Alert, active minds were at work in the world, finding themselves always at ease, sending forth a spiritual light and warmth that melted the oppressive coils round the souls of those adults who came into contact with them. These children welcomed all with love. It was thus that important people began to pay them visits to receive new, refreshing impressions, and the children became the centre of an intense social life. It was curious to see how even ordinary visitors began to show feelings quite other than what was usual with them. Ladies, for example, would put on their most elegant clothes and jewellery, as if to call on some one they wished to honour, and they rejoiced in the admiration of the children, so fresh and naive, and devoid of envy; they were happy to hear how the little ones expressed their compliments.

The children stroked the fine stuffs and the soft perfumed hands of such ladies. Once a little boy went up to a lady in deep mourning and leant his head against her, then he took her hand and held it between his own. She said afterwards with much emotion that no one had given her such comfort as that child.

## Spontaneous Discipline

In spite of this ease and freedom of manner, the children as a whole gave an impression of extraordinary discipline. They worked quietly, each one intent on his own task; they went about walking quietly, to get fresh work or to put back what they had been doing. They went out of the room, gave a glance at the courtyard, and came back. They fulfilled the wishes expressed by their teacher with an amazing rapidity. She told me, "They are so ready to do what I say that I begin to feel a sense of responsibility for every word I utter." Indeed, if she wanted to ask them, to do the silence exercise, the words were not out of her mouth before the children all sat motionless. "We shall now keep still...." In spite of this apparent dependence, they knew how to act on their own, arranging their own time and their day. They took their own material, put the school tidy, and if the teacher came late, or went out leaving them alone, everything went just as well. This indeed was the chief attraction for those who observed them—order and discipline combined with spontaneity.

Whence came this perfect discipline, so apparent even when it showed itself in deep silence, this obedience that made them so ready to do what they were told, even before it had been told, guessed rather than heard? The quiet in class was complete when the children were at work and moving. No one had enforced it, and what is more, no one could have obtained it by external means. Had these children may be found the orbit of their cycle, like stars that circle unwearying and which without departing from their order shine through eternity? Of these the Bible speaks, in words that could be applied to such children, "And the stars have given light in their watches and rejoiced; their fullness they have shined forth to Him that made them." A natural discipline of this kind seems to transcend its immediate environment, and to show itself as part of a universal discipline ruling the world. It is of such discipline that the prophet speaks as of something men have lost. "Young men have seen the light and dwelt upon the earth, but the way of discipline they have not known." One has the impression that this natural discipline must provide the foundation for all other forms of discipline determined—like that of social life, for instance—by outward and immediate considerations. One of the things, indeed, which aroused the greatest interest and gave greatest food for thought, seeming as it did to hold something mysterious, was precisely this fact of order and discipline so closely united as to result in freedom.

One day a lady, the daughter of our Prime Minister, wished to accompany the Argentine Ambassador on a visit to the *Casa dei Bambini,* The Ambassador had decided to give no warning of his visit, so that he might see the *spontaneity* of which he had been told. But, when he arrived, he learned that the day was a holiday and that the school was closed. In the courtyard were some of the children, who at once came up to him. "It doesn't matter if it is a holiday," said one, quite naturally, "for we are all at home, and the porter has the key." They began to run about calling their comrades by names, and, having got the door open, all sat down to work. Thus their marvellous spontaneity was proved beyond all question.

The children's mothers were aware of such acts. It can be imagined how amazed were the families in the tenement when they saw the visitors who came into the courtyard to see their children—the Queen of Italy, the King himself, and a number of exalted personages they had never expected to see even from a distance. But it was not of this that they used to talk to me. They came instead to confide intimate family details. "These little ones of three and four," they told me, "say things to us that would offend us from anyone else. They say, for instance, 'You've got dirty hands, you ought to wash them. You ought to wash the spots on your dress.' When we hear this from them, we aren't offended. They tell us of things just like in dreams." The fact was that all these working people were becoming cleaner and tidier. Broken saucepans began to disappear from the window sills. Little by little the windows became clean and geraniums appeared on the sills round the courtyard. But the most impressive fact was that often some poor woman would put on the school window sill, which was on the ground floor, some favourite dish she had cooked and which she wished to offer the mistress as a sign of gratitude, without letting her know who had given it.

## "I've **Written!** I've **Written!**"

Once two or three mothers came to me in a deputation, asking me to teach their children how to read and write. They themselves were illiterate. And as I made objections, feeling that such an undertaking was out of my scope, they begged me insistently.

It was then that the most surprising things of all happened. All I taught the children of four and five was some of the letters of the alphabet, which I made the mistress cut out of cardboard. I also had some cut out of sand-paper, so that the children could touch them with their finger-tips, feeling out the shapes as for writing; these I also arranged on a board, putting together the letters of similar shape so that the movement of the little hands should be uniform. The mistress liked the idea, and was content to remain at this primitive beginning.

I could not understand why the children were so keen: they made processions carrying the letters aloft like banners with shouts of joy. Why? One day I surprised a child who was walking by himself repeating, "To make *sofia* you need S, O, F, I, A," and he repeated the sound making up the word. He was engaged in a study, analysing the words, he had in his mind and hunting for the sounds of which they were composed.

With the profound interest of one who has made a discovery, he had understood that each of these sounds corresponded to a letter of the alphabet. Indeed, what is alphabetical writing, if not the correspondence of a sign with a sound? Language in itself is spoken language; written language is nothing else than a really *literal* translation. All the progress of alphabetical writing springs from this point of contact from which the two languages can evolve in parallel. In the beginning the one, the written language, falls from the other drop by drop, and these will later form a distinct stream, words and discourse.

Here is a real secret, a key which, once discovered, brings a two-fold gain. It allows the hand to master a vital, almost unconscious labour, such as spoken language, and to create another language reflecting it in every detail. Head and hand are both the gainers. The hand gives a fresh impetus, and the drops become a waterfall. The whole language comes to have its written counterpart. For it is a stream, a waterfall, and yet made up of little drops of sound.

Once an alphabet has been formed, written language should derive from it logically, as a natural consequence. For this, the hand must have the ability to trace signs. Alphabetical signs which are mere symbols making no attempt at representation are, therefore, very easy to draw. But on all these things I had never reflected when the greatest event of all took place in the *Casa dei Bambini*.

One day a child began to write. He was so astonished that he shouted aloud, "I've written! I've written!" Other children rushed up to him, full of interest, staring at the words that their play-fellow had traced on the ground with a piece of white chalk. "I too! I too!" shouted the others, and ran off. They ran to find a means of writing; some crowded round a blackboard, others stretched themselves on the ground, and thus written language began to develop as an *explosion*. This tireless activity was truly like a torrent. They wrote everywhere—on doors, walls, and even at home on loaves of bread. They were about four years old. The discovery of being able to write appeared as an unexpected event. The teacher would tell me, for instance, "This child began to write yesterday at 3 p.m."

We felt as though we were in the presence of a miracle. But when we gave books to the children (and many people who had heard of what had happened brought us some very fine picture books), these books were coldly received, as things with pretty pictures but distracting from the enthralling and wholly absorbing task of writing. Perhaps, those children had never seen books, but for a long time we tried in vain to make them take an interest in them. It was not even possible to make them understand what reading meant. So we put the books away, till a more propitious time. They did not even read what was written by hand. It was rare for one of them to bother to read what another had written; indeed, they seemed incapable of reading the word. Many children turned round to look at me with astonishment when I read aloud the words they had written, as though they asked, "How do you know?"

## Reading Came Later

It was about six months later that they began to understand what reading meant, and they did so only through associating it with writing. Their eyes followed my hand as it traced the signs on paper, and they grasped the idea that thus I was expressing my thoughts as if I were speaking. Barely had this idea become clear when they seized the pieces of paper on which I had written, to carry them off to a corner and try to read them, and they read them mentally, without pronouncing a sound. One knew that they had understood from the smile that suddenly appeared on the small face for a moment, earlier contracted by effort, or from a little jump that seemed evoked by a hidden spring. Then they would go about. For each sentence I had written was an order, such as I might have made by word of mouth. "Open the window," "Come close to me," etc. That was how they began to read. Soon they were able to read long sentences, ordering complicated actions. But it seemed that written language was understood by children merely as another way of expressing themselves, another form of spoken language meant in the same way to be transmitted directly from one person to another.

Indeed now when visitors came, many children who had earlier exceeded in vocal greeting were silent. They got up and went to write on the blackboard, "Take a seat, thank you for the visit," etc. Once they were told of a terrible disaster in Sicily, where an earthquake had utterly destroyed the city of Messina, leaving hundreds of thousands of victims. A child about five years old got up and went to write on the blackboard. He began thus: "I am sorry...." We watched him, expecting he would say he was sorry about the disaster. Instead he wrote: "I am sorry that

I am little." It seemed a strangely egotistical reflection. But he went on: "If I was big I should go to help." He had made a little composition, revealing at the same time his generous heart. He was the son of a woman who kept him by selling herbs in a basket in the street.

Later on, something equally surprising happened. While we were preparing materials for teaching the printed alphabet, in order to give the books another try, the children began to read all the printed matter in the school. Some of this was really difficult to decipher, such as a calendar on which words were printed in gothic lettering. At the same time their parents came to tell us that in the street the children would stop to read shop-signs, so that it was impossible to go out for walks with them. It was plain that the children were interested not in reading the words, but in puzzling out the alphabetical signs. Here was another form of writing which they wished to learn, and they could do so precisely by elucidating the sense of the words. Their minds were working in the same way as that of the adult who pores over a prehistoric inscription, till the sense he gathers from it proves to him that he has correctly deciphered the signs he did not know. The children's sudden, passionate interest in anything in print sprang from such a motive.

If we had been in too much of a hurry to explain the printed characters, we should have quenched their interest and eagerness to puzzle out the unfamiliar. An untimely insistence on their reading words from books would have been the reverse of helpful; by presenting an unimportant finality it would have diminished the energy of those dynamic minds.

And so the books remained for a further period shut up in the cupboards. It was only later that the children came into relationship with books. It began with a really thrilling event. A child came to school full of excitement, hiding in his hand a crumpled piece of paper, and confided to a friend, "Guess what's in this piece of paper." "There's nothing; it's a torn bit of paper." "No, there's a story...." "A story in it?" This at once drew an interested crowd. The child had picked up the paper from a rubbish heap. And he began to read the story. Then at last they grasped the significance of books, and after this, the books went like hot cakes. But many of the children, when they found an interesting story, tore out the page and carried it away.

Those books! The discovery of their value was truly staggering. The habitual peaceful order of the school was overthrown, and it was necessary to control those eager little hands that destroyed out of pure love. Even before they could read the books and learn to respect them, the children, with some help, had learned to spell correctly, and they wrote so well that they could be compared to children in Class III of the primary schools.

## New Children

During all this time nothing had been done to improve the physical conditions of the children. But now no one would have recognised in their rosy faces and their alert looks the underfed anaemic children who had seemed in urgent need of medical care, food, and tonics. They were as healthy as if they had completed an open air and sun cure. Indeed, if depressive psychological causes can have an influence on the metabolism so as to lower vitality, the contrary can come about, that is, stimulating psychological causes can increase the activity of the metabolism and of all physical functions. Of this we had here a proof. Today this would not create any surprise, but in those days it aroused amazement.

All this made people talk of "miracles", and so eloquently did the press speak of them that the news of the wonderful children spread in a trice all over the world. Books were written on those children; they inspired novelists who, in giving exact descriptions of what they had seen, seemed to be depicting an unknown world. People spoke of the discovery of the human soul, they spoke of miracles, they quoted child conversions. The latest English book dealing with them is called *New Children*. From distant countries, and especially from America, many people came to verify the surprising facts. Our children might well have repeated the Biblical words that are read in church on January 6th, the feast of the Magi, the day of the opening of the school: "Lift up thine eyes round about and see: all these are gathered together: They are come to thee... the multitude from beyond the sea shall be converted to thee."

# 8

# Further Developments

## THE PRINCIPLES ESTABLISHED

This brief account of incidents and impressions will have thrown little light on the question of "method." By what method were such results obtained?

Here is the point.

One cannot see the method; *one sees the child.* One sees the child soul, freed from obstacles, acting in accordance with its true nature. The child qualities of which we catch glimpses are simply a part of *life,* like the colours of birds or the scent of flowers; they are not at all the results of any "method of education." But it is evident that these natural facts can be influenced by an education seeking to protect them, cultivate them, and assist their development. Even on flowers, with their natural colours and scents, man can exercise an influence by cultivation; he can ensure the appearance of certain characters, and he can cause the primary characters presented by nature to develop in strength and beauty. Now the phenomena presented in a *Casa dei Bambini* are natural psychological characteristics. They are not apparent like the natural facts of vegetative life, for psychic life is so fluid that its characteristics may completely disappear in an unfavourable environment, to be replaced by others. Therefore, before proceeding to educative development, it is necessary to establish the conditions of an environment that will favour the emergence of the normal hidden characteristics. To this end it is enough to *remove obstacles,* this is the first step and the foundation of education. It is thus a question not merely of developing existing characteristics, but first of discovering the real nature of the child; only afterwards does it become possible to foster normal development.

If we study the first series of conditions, produced by chance, and which led to the emergence of normal characteristics, we may note a few of especial importance. One is the provision of a pleasant environment, where the children felt no constraint. Those children who had come from wretched hovels must have found their new environment very pleasant indeed—the clean, white room, the new little tables, the new little chairs, and armchairs, made on purpose for them, and the little lawns of the sunny courtyard.

Another condition was the *negative* role of the adult—illiterate parents, a working-class mistress without the ambitions or prejudices of a real school teacher. Here was a situation that might be considered one of "intellectual calm." It has always been recognised that a teacher must be calm, but the calm demanded was one of character and nerves. Here was a deeper calm; a state of emptiness or (better) of freedom from mental lumber, producing an inner translucency, a freedom from intellectual attachment. Such a state approaches the intellectual purity that St. Francis of Assisi felt, and which was confused with ignorance, whereas it was a mental state predisposing to that *illuminative* state open to divine enlightenment. Similar to this is the *spiritual humility* which prepares us to understand the child, and which should, therefore, be the most essential part of a teacher's preparation.

Another notable circumstance was the provision of suitable and alluring scientific material for the children, perfected with a view to sensorial education, of such things as the lacing frames, which allowed an analysis and refinement of movements. All these were such as to awaken concentrated attention. This could never have come about if someone like a teacher teaching by word of mouth had called forth their energies from the outside.

So far we have a suitable environment, humility in the teacher, and scientific material. Here are the three external features of the method.

Let us now seek to discover some of the manifestations on the part of the children.

The most pertinent, which seemed like a magic touch opening the gates to an expansion of normal characteristics, is a consistent activity concentrated on a single work, an exercise on some external object, where the movements of the hands are guided by the mind. And here we find the unfolding of characteristics which plainly come from an inner impulse, like the "repetition of the exercise" and "free choice of objects". It is then that the true child appears, aglow with joy, indefatigable because his activity is like the psychic metabolism to which life and hence development is attached. From now on it is his own choice that guides him. He responds eagerly to certain tests, like that of silence; he delights in certain lessons which open a way of justice and dignity before him. He avidly assimilates the means that enable him to develop his mind. Whereas he turns from other things, such as prizes, sweets, and toys. Moreover, he shows us that order and discipline are vital needs and a vital expression where he is concerned. And all the while he is a real child, fresh, sincere, gay, lively, shouting when his enthusiasm overflows, applauding, greeting loudly, thanking with effusion, calling and running after one in sign of gratitude. He approaches all, admires everything, adapts himself to everything.

Let us choose out, then, the things that he has chosen, and let us take into account his spontaneous manifestations in order to make a kind of list. And at the same time let us note the things he has rejected, listing them, to avoid wasting time, as things abolished.

The first list shows us: Individual work. Repetition of the exercise. Free choice. Control of error. Analysis of movements. Silence exercises. Good manners in social contacts. Order in the environment. Meticulous personal cleanliness. Sense education. Writing isolated from reading. Writing prior to reading. Reading without books. Discipline in free activity.

And then the second list: Abolition of rewards and punishments. Abolition of A. B. C. Abolition of collective lessons.[1] Abolition of programmes and examinations. Abolition of toys and greediness. Abolition of a special high desk for the teacher.

Undoubtedly, in this double list we find the outline of an educational method. In short, practical and positive, or rather experimental guiding lines have been provided by the child himself for the construction of

---

[1] This does not mean that no collective lessons are given in the Houses of Children, only that they are neither the only nor the main means of teaching. They are a means reserved for special topics and activities.

a method of education, in which his choice guides its shaping and his vital eagerness acts as a control of error.

It is indeed marvellous to realise that in the subsequent building up of a real method of education, worked out by the experiences of a long period, these early principles that came from nothing have remained intact. It makes one think of the embryo of a vertebrate, in which a line appears that is known as the primitive line: it is a real design without substance, which will later become the vertebral column. We may carry the comparison further. In the vertebrate we see the whole divided into three parts—head, thoracic section, abdominal section; then a number of points that little by little follow an ordered evolution and end by solidifying—the vertebrae. Thus in the primary outline of our educational method there is a whole, a basic line on which three essential factors stand out—the environment, the teacher and the apparatus, with a number of special features that evolve little by little, like the vertebrae.

It would be interesting to follow this elaboration step by step, the first work in human society guided by the child, showing the evolution of those principles that presented themselves at first as unsuspected revelations. Evolution is the best term to indicate the successive developments of this singular method; for new details were produced by life as it evolved at the expense of its environment. This environment, however, is a special one, for it too, through the work of the adult, is an active and vital response to the new patterns revealed by the evolution of child life.

The extraordinary rapid spread of attempts to apply this method to schools for children of every social condition and even of every race, has so widened our experience as to enable us to note beyond all question the existence of constant features, of universal tendencies, and thus, we may say, of *natural laws* which should form the first basis of education.

The schools that followed the first *Casa dei Bambini* are especially interesting through the fact that they were inspired by the same principle of awaiting the children's spontaneous manifestations, before an external preparation of definite methods had been established.

## MESSINA ORPHANS

An impressive and indeed celebrated example was obtained in one of the first *Casa dei Bambini* to be founded in Rome. The circumstances were still more unusual than in the case of the first school, because here were orphans who had survived one of the greatest catastrophes, the Messina earthquake (1908), sixty small children discovered among the ruins. No one knew either their names or their social status. This terrible shock had reduced them to near uniformity, they were numbed, silent, absent-minded. It was hard to make them eat, hard to get them to sleep. At night they could be heard screaming and crying.

A delightful environment was prepared for them, and the Queen of Italy made them her personal concern. Little pieces of furniture were made, gaily coloured and of every kind, little cupboards, bright curtains, little round tables, very low and brightly painted, higher rectangular tables, little upright chairs and armchairs. The dinner service was particularly attractive. The plates were tiny, so were the utensils and napkins, and even cakes of soap and towels were all in proportion to small hands that would take long to grow to full size. On everything there was an ornament, a sign of refinement. There were pretty pictures on the walls and vases of flowers everywhere. The place chosen was a convent of Franciscan nuns, with big gardens and wide paths. They grew flowers; there were ponds of gold-fish and dove-cots. In this setting the nuns, in their light-coloured habits, majestic in their long veils, moved in calm and silence.

They taught the children good manners, with increasing insistence on detail. Many came from the aristocracy, and these put into practice the most meticulous usages of the society life they had left, searching in memory and early habits for any details they could recall, for the children seemed insatiable. They learned to behave at table like princes, and they also learned to wait at table like the best waiters. The dinner that no longer attracted them as food attracted them through a spirit of exactitude, as an exercise in controlled movements, through uplifting facts of knowledge, and little by little the children also regained the hearty appetites natural to their age, together with tranquil sleep. The change in them was really impressive. You saw them running and jumping, as they carried things into the garden, moving furniture of a room to put it in a little square under the trees, without breaking anything or knocking into anything, their faces alert and joyous. It was here that the term "conversion" was first applied. "These children seem to me as if they had experienced conversion," said a lady who was one of the most distinguished Italian authoresses of the time; "there is no conversion more miraculous than that which vanquishes melancholy and depression, and brings an entry to a higher plane of life." This idea, which gave a spiritual form to the inexplicable and impressive phenomena that none could fail to recognise, stirred many minds, and the term remained in vogue for a long time in spite of its paradoxical sense. For the idea of conversion seems contrary to the state of innocence of childhood. But here was a spiritual change, by which they were liberated from sorrow and abandonment and reborn to joy. Sadness and sin are both conditions that indicate a remoteness from the fount of vital energies, and, under this aspect, to be able to rediscover such vital energies is to be converted. Then sadness and guilt disappear like the night, and the day dawns in joy and purification. Indeed, the two things are implied among the gifts of the Holy Spirit. He is called "highest Comforter," "sweet refreshment," "rest in labour," "comfort in weeping." He purges what is ugly, waters what is dry, heals what is wounded, bends what is rigid, straightens the crooked, and gives health and perpetual joy. There is nothing in man without His aid, nothing without Him that is not harmful.[2]

Truly, this was what was happening to our children. There was a resurrection from sadness to joy, with the disappearance of many faults

---

[2] From the Whitsun Sequence, variously attributed to King Robert of France, Stephen Langton and Pope Innocent III:

> *Consolator optime,*
> > *Dulcis hospes animae,*
> > *Dulce refrigerium.*
> *In labore requies,*
> > *In aestu temperies,*
> > *In fletu solatium....*
> *Sine too numine,*
> > *Nihil est in homine,*
> > *Nihil est innoxium.*
> *Lava quod est sordidum,*
> > *Riga quod est aridum,*
> > *Sana quod est saucium,*
> *Flecte quod est rigidum,*
> > *Fove quod est frigidum,*
> > *Rege quod est devium....*

—TRANSLATOR'S NOTE

that are usually feared because considered incorrigible, but there was something more—the disappearance also of characteristics that are usually looked upon as merits. Here indeed the children brought a dazzling enlightenment. *Nihil est innoxium....* Everything in man is mistaken and everything must be made new. And for this remaking there is only one way—a return to the sole source of creative energies. Without this complex demonstration in the children who came to our schools from the most abnormal conditions of life it would not have been possible to distinguish good and evil in the characters of children; for previously the adult had made up his own mind that the child was good in so far as he adapted himself to the adult's conditions of life, and vice versa. Through these opposing judgments the natural characteristics of the child had remained buried. The real child had disappeared; he was an unknown in the adult world; good and evil kept him buried alike.

### WELL-TO-DO CHILDREN

Another class of children who live in exceptional social conditions is that of the children of the rich. One would imagine they would be much easier to educate than the very poor children of the first school, or the orphans from the Messina earthquake. In what, indeed, could their conversion consist? Rich children are privileged children, surrounded by every care society can provide. But to clear up this prejudice I will quote a few pages from an old book of mine,[3] in which teachers who worked in our schools in Europe and America give a sincere account of their first impressions and the difficulties they encountered, making one think of the words of St. Francis when he extols humble things: "Draw near, Sister Grasshopper; it is in the smallest creatures that the goodness of the Creator is best revealed."

Beauty in his environment, a wealth of flowers, do not attract the rich child. The garden paths do not allure him. The correspondence between child and apparatus is not reached. The teacher is disoriented by the fact that the children do not fling themselves, as she will have hoped, on the

---

3 Dr. Maria Montessori: *The Advanced Montessori Method,* Vol. I, pp. 72–78 (Publ. Kalakshetra, Madras-600020).

objects she presents, choosing among them as their preferences direct. In schools for poor children this nearly always happens from the very first. But rich children, already satiated with objects of every kind and with magnificent toys, rarely feel an attraction to the stimuli presented to them.

An American teacher, Miss G., wrote from Washington: "The children snatched the apparatus from each other; if I tried to show something to one child, the others dropped what they were doing and noisily, without any purpose, gathered round me. When I had finished explaining an apparatus, all crowded round it and fought for it. The children showed no interest in the apparatus. They passed from one thing to another without persisting in any. There was a child so incapable of keeping still that he could not sit down long enough to pass his fingers over one of the small objects we give to the children. In many cases the movements of the children held no purpose. They ran round the room without any end in mind. In moving they took no care to respect things, they ran into the table, upset the chairs, and walked on the apparatus. Sometimes they began to work at something in one place, then ran somewhere else, picked up another object, only to leave it."

Mlle. D. wrote from Paris: "I must confess that my experiences were really discouraging. The children could not concentrate on any work for more than a minute. They had no perseverance, and no initiative. Often they just followed one another like a flock of lambs. When a child picked up an object, all the others wanted to imitate. Sometimes they rolled on the ground and upset the chairs."

From a school for rich children in Rome comes the following laconic description: "The chief concern is discipline. The children are disoriented in their work, and refractory to guidance."

Here now are some descriptions of the advent of discipline. Miss G. gave the following account of her experiences in Washington: "In a few days that nebulous mass of whirling particles (the disorderly children) began to assume a definite shape. The children seemed to begin to find their own orientation; they began to take an original interest in many objects that they had begun by despising as silly toys, and as a result of this new interest they began to act as independent individuals, *very highly individualised.* It then came about that an object absorbing the whole attention of one child had not the smallest attraction for another; the children divided from each other in their manifestations of attention.

"The battle is really won only when the child discovers something, some particular object, which *arouses in him a deep and spontaneous interest.* Sometimes this enthusiasm is born suddenly, with strange rapidity. I had once tried in vain to interest a child, showing him every piece of apparatus, without arousing a spark of attention. Then, by chance, I showed him two red and blue tablets, calling his attention to the difference of colour. He took them at once with a kind of hunger and learned five colours in one lesson. In the following days he took all the pieces of apparatus which he had at first scorned, and little by little became interested in all.

"A child who had at first very slight power of concentration found a way out of this state of chaos through becoming interested in one of the most complicated pieces of apparatus, the so-called number-rods. He worked with them continually for a week on end, and learned to count and to do simple additions. Then he began to work backwards, the simpler objects, the cylinders, the metal insets, and came to take interest in every part of the apparatus.

"No sooner do the children find the objects that interest them than disorder disappears in a flash and the wanderings of their minds are at an end."

The same teacher describes an awakening of personality. "There were two sisters, one of three and the other of five. The child of three did not exist as an individuality at all, for she copied her elder sister exactly in everything. If her sister had a blue pencil, the little one would not rest content till she had a blue one too; if her sister ate bread and butter and she had something different, she would insist on bread and butter and so on. This little girl showed no interest in anything in the school but simply imitated her elder sister in everything she did. One day the little one became interested in the pink cubes. She built her tower, and her interest became very keen. She repeated the exercise many times and completely forgot her sister. The elder sister was so surprised that she called her and said: 'How is it I'm filling a circle and you're building the tower?' From that day forth the little one showed a personality of her own and began to develop on her own. She was no longer just the mirror of her sister."

Mile. D. speaks of a little girl of four who was absolutely incapable of carrying a glass of water, even though it were only half full, without spilling, so much so that she avoided attempting it in the knowledge that she could not do it. She developed an interest in an exercise of another kind with one of the apparatus, and after that she began to carry glasses of water with the greatest of ease. And since some of her school-fellows were painting in water-colour, it became a craze with her to carry water to all, without spilling a drop. Another really curious fact was reported by an Australian teacher, Miss B. She had in her school a little girl who had not yet developed the power of speech, and who uttered only inarticulate sounds, so that her parents had had her medically examined to find out if she were abnormal. This little girl one day took an interest in the solid cylinders, spending a long time working with them, pulling the little wooden cylinders out of their holes and putting them in again. And after she had repeated her task a great many times with the keenest interest, she ran to the teacher saying, "Come and look!"

Miss B. tells of the children's joy in their work. "The children showed the pride we feel when we have produced something really new by ourselves. They danced about and threw their arms round my neck when they had learned to do something very simple, and they told me: 'I've done it all myself. You didn't think that I could do this, did you? And to-day I've done it better than yesterday'."

Mile. D. says: "After the Christmas holidays, there was a great change in the class. It seemed that order established itself without any intervention of mine. The children seemed too busy with their work for the disorderly actions they had engaged in before. They went by themselves to the cupboard to choose the objects that had earlier seemed boring to them, and they took them one after another, without showing any sign of tiredness. An atmosphere of work spread through the class. The children who till then had taken up objects only through the whim of the moment, felt now, as it were, the need for a kind of rule, for a personal inner rule; they concentrated their efforts on accurate and methodical tasks, feeling a real satisfaction in overcoming difficulties. This accurate work produced an immediate result on their characters. They became their own masters."

The example that most struck Mile. D. was that of a little boy of four and a half, who had an extremely vivid imagination, so much so that when he was given an object he did not observe its shape but personified it, and at the same time personified himself, talking continually, imagining himself someone else, and it was impossible to make him fix his attention on the objects themselves. While his mind was thus distracted he was incapable of any precise action, such as doing up even one button. All at once something marvellous began to work in him. "I saw," she says, "with amazement how a remarkable change came over him. He took one of the exercises as his favourite occupation, and afterwards passed on to all the others. And thus he became calm."

## TRUE NORMALITY

These old, authentic descriptions by teachers who opened schools before a sure method had been established, could be repeated almost *ad infinitum,* always the same. Similar incidents and similar difficulties, though in a lesser degree, are to be found with nearly all *happy* children who have intelligent and loving families to look after them. There are spiritual difficulties bound up with what we call prosperity, and which explain how the famous words of the Sermon on the Mount find an echo in every heart: "Blessed are the poor in spirit, blessed are they that weep."

But all are called, all are able to respond, overcoming their particular difficulties. Hence the phenomenon that was called "conversion" is proper to childhood. It implies a swift, sometimes instantaneous change, brought about always by the same cause. It would not be possible to quote a single example of conversion that did not involve the concentration of activity on an interesting task. And the conversions that thus come about are of widely differing kinds. Children of excited fantasy become calm, depressed children rise up, and all advance together, on the same road of work and discipline, continuing a progress which evolves of itself, moved by some inner energy that, having found a way of egress, can display itself in outward act.

There is an explosive character in facts that arise suddenly as sure heralds of a development that will follow after. It is the same as when one day, of a sudden, a tooth appears, just as of a sudden the baby utters his first word, or takes his first step. When the first tooth has appeared, the whole set of teeth will follow; after the first word, speech develops, after the first step, the art of walking is permanently acquired.

Thus development had been arrested, or rather, had been turned into a wrong direction, in *all children,* in children of every social condition. The spread of our schools over the world, among every race, proved this child conversion to be a general fact, common to all mankind. It became possible to make a meticulous study of an innumerable *quantity* of characteristics that fade away, to be replaced always by the same structure of life. Thus, at the origin of life, in the small child, errors are constantly being made, deforming the natural psychological type of man, and leading to an infinity of *deviations.*

The singular fact that we note in child conversions is a psychological recovery, a return to *normal conditions.* The child who seems miraculous in his precocious intelligence, the hero who overcomes himself and his own grief, finding strength to live and new serenity, the rich child who prefers disciplined work to frivolities of life, are *normal children.* And that which was called conversion when it implied only the emergence of a surprising fact must, after the finding of wide experience, be reckoned a *normalization.* There was a hidden nature in man, a nature buried and, therefore, unknown, which none the less is simply his true nature, the nature given by creation, health.

This interpretation does not cancel the features of conversion; perhaps even the adult can be summoned back to what he should be, but this is so difficult that such a change could not be considered a mere return to human nature. Whereas in the child the normal psychic characteristics can easily emerge, and then all the conditions that were deviations from the norm disappear together, just as with restored health all the symptoms of illness vanish. If we observe children in the light of this understanding, we should very often be able to recognise spontaneous emergences of normality even where the conditions of environment are difficult. And, though driven under because unrecognised and unassisted, they return, as vital energies that make a place for themselves in the midst of obstacles, seeking to prevail. It might be said that the normal energies of the child teach us a lesson of forgiveness, as in the words of Christ: "Thou shalt not forgive seven times, but seventy times seven." Thus the deeper nature of the child returns to the surface not seven times but seventy times seven, however it be repressed by the adult. It is, therefore, not a transitory episode of infant life that engulfs the characteristics of normality, but a struggle due to continuous repression.

# 9

# Psychic Deviations

## THEIR SINGLE CAUSE

Observing the features that disappear with normalization, we find to our surprise that these embrace nearly the whole of what are considered characteristics of childhood. Not only untidiness, disobedience, laziness, greediness, selfishness, quarrelling, naughtiness, but also so-called creative imagination, delight in stories, attachment to persons, submissiveness, play, etc. Even the features that have been scientifically studied as proper to childhood, such as imitation, curiosity, inconstancy, instability of attention, disappear. And this means that the nature of the child, as hitherto known, is a mere semblance masking an original and normal nature. Here is a fact the more striking in that it is universal, but it is nothing new. From earliest antiquity it has been recognised that there are two natures in man—man as he was created, and man as fallen, the fall being attributed to an original error affecting all mankind: original sin. It has also been recognised that this sin in itself is trivial, out of all proportion to the immensity of its consequences, but implying a forsaking of the creative spirit, of the laws laid down in creation. After it man becomes like a drifting ship, driven by chance, with no defence against the obstacles of his environment or against the illusions of his mind. Hence he is lost. This conception, a synthesis of the philosophy of life, finds a singular and illuminating counterpart in the life of the child. A very trivial thing leads to deviation, something hidden and tenuous that creeps in under the guise of love and help, but which at bottom comes from a blindness in the adult soul, a veiled and unconscious egotism, that is really a diabolical power working against the child. But the child is continually reborn, fresh and bearing in himself intact the pattern which should determine the development of the man.

If normalization comes about through a determined and single fact, viz. the concentration on some activity of movement, which brings the child into relation with external reality, we must suppose that a single fact lies at the source of all deviation, viz. that the child has been prevented from fulfilling the original pattern of his development, through some action affecting his environment at the formative age, when his potential energies should evolve through a process of *incarnation.*

If we are thus able to reduce a host of consequences to a single, clear and simple cause, it proves that the fact from which they derive must belong to a primary period of life, when man is still a spiritual embryo; then this single, imperceptible cause may lead to distortion of the whole being.

## FUGUES

As a guide in interpreting the characteristics resulting from deviation, we may, therefore, take the idea of *incarnation*—of a psychic energy that must achieve incarnation through movement, thus welding the acting personality into unity. If this unity cannot be achieved, through the substitution of the adult for the child or through a want of motives of activity in his environment, psychic energy and movement must develop separately, and a "broken man" results. Since in nature nothing creates itself and nothing destroys itself, and this is especially true in the case of energies, these energies, since they have to work outside the scope assigned to them by nature, become deviated. They are deviated because above all they have lost their object and work in emptiness, vagueness and chaos. The mind that should have built itself up through experiences of movement, *flees* into fantasy. Such fugitive minds began by seeking and not finding, they wished to attach themselves to things and could not, and thus they wander among images and symbols. As for movement, these lively children are never still, but their movements are disordered, without purpose. They begin an action only to leave it unfinished, for their energy passes through things without becoming fixed on any. The adult, even while he punishes the unregulated and disturbing actions of such sturdy, restless children, or while he bears them by exercise of patience, none the less admires and encourages their fancies, interpreting them as imagination, as the creative fecundity of the child mind. It is well known that many of Froebel's gifts and pastimes are intended to encourage the development of such symbolism. He helps the child to pretend that his blocks and bricks variously assembled are horses or castles or trains. Indeed, the child's tendency to symbolism leads him to use any object as though it were an electric switch illuminating the fantastic mirages of his mind. A stick is a horse, a chair a throne, a pencil, an aeroplane. That is why children are given toys, which do not allow them to exercise any real activity, but provide them with ideas and illusions. They are merely imperfect and unproductive images of reality. Toys, in fact, seem to present a useless environment which cannot lead to any concentration of the spirit and which has no purpose; they are for minds astray in illusion. Toys immediately stir children to activity, like an animating breath that brings to flame a glowing coal hidden under ashes. But almost at once the flame goes out and the toy is thrown away. And yet toys are the only things that the adult has made for the child as an intelligent being, in the endeavour to provide him with material on which his activity can be freely exercised. The adult in fact leaves the child free only in his games, or better, only with his toys, in the conviction that these form a world in which he will be happy. This conviction has persisted, even though the child soon tires of his toys and so often breaks them, but here the adult has shown himself generous and liberal, and the gift of toys becomes a ritual. It is the only freedom that the adult world has allowed to man in the venerable age of infancy, at a time when he should be setting the roots of a higher life. Such "broken" children are considered very intelligent, especially at school, but undisciplined and disorderly. But in our specially prepared environments we see them all at once fix themselves upon some task, and then their excited fantasies and their restless movements disappear together; a calm, serene child, attached to reality, begins to work out his elevation through work. Normalization has been achieved. His organs of movement have emerged from chaos in the moment in which they were able to attach themselves to their inward guide; henceforth they will become the instruments of an intelligence hungry to know and to penetrate the reality of the outer world. And this wandering curiosity is transformed into an effort to master knowledge.

Psycho-analysis has recognised the abnormal side of imagination and play, and by a luminous interpretation has registered them among "psychological fugues". A fugue is a running away, a taking refuge and often hiding away of an energy that is out of its natural place; or else it represents a subconscious defence of the ego, which flies from discomfort or danger and hides itself behind a mask.

## "BARRIERS"

In school teachers notice that highly imaginative children are not the ones that succeed in gaining the most profit from their studies, as might have been expected. Indeed they seem sometimes to gain hardly any or no profit at all. Yet no one suspects that there has been a deviation of their intelligence; it is believed that a great creative intelligence cannot apply itself to practical things. Here is one of the plainest signs; that the deviated child has a *diminished intelligence;* for he does not possess his mind, nor can he lead it towards its full development. This happens not only where the mind has taken refuge in a world of illusion, but also in many other cases in which, on the contrary, intelligence has been more or less suppressed and quenched in discouragement—where instead of fleeing without, it has withdrawn itself within. The average intelligence level of ordinary children is *low,* compared with that of normalized children. This comes about through deviations that might be compared, roughly, to dislocated bones, out of place, and hence requiring most delicate care if there is to be a return to normality. Whereas the usual method is one of direct aggression, both in intellectual teaching and in correction of disorder. It is impossible to constrain a deviated intelligence to forced labour, without encountering or rather provoking a defence that, as a psychological phenomenon, is most interesting. It is not the defence that is by now well known to psychology in general, and which shows itself outwardly as disobedience or obstinacy. It is, on the contrary, a psychic defence wholly outside the domain of the will, and it represents a subconscious impediment to the reception, and hence to the comprehension, of ideas imposed from without. It is akin to the phenomenon to which psycho-analysts have given the descriptive name of inhibitions. The teacher should recognise these grave facts. A kind of curtain comes down over the child's mind, making him psychologically ever more deaf and blind. It is as though the subconscious mind were to say: "You speak, but I am not listening; you repeat things, but I do not hear you. I cannot build up my world because I am building up a wall of defence so that you cannot come in!"

This slow, prolonged work of defence leads a child to act as though he had lost his natural powers, and here it is no longer a question of willingness or unwillingness. The teacher who has to do with pupils in whom such psychic barriers exist will think them unintelligent, or naturally incapable of understanding certain subjects, for instance, mathematics, or of correcting their spelling mistakes. If such psychic barriers cover many subjects, or as sometimes happens, all subjects, intelligent children may be confused with defectives, and after remaining in the same class for several years may be definitely relegated among the backward children. As a rule the psychic barrier is not only an impenetrability; but carries with it coefficients that work at a distance. Thus we find repugnance to a special subject, then repugnance to study in general, to the school, the teacher, the other children. There is no more room for love or cordiality, till the child comes to be afraid of school, and then he is wholly cut off.

Nothing is more common than for individuals to carry psychic barriers set up in infancy throughout their lives. We find an example in the typical repugnance to mathematics that many feel all their lives. It is not only an incapacity to understand, but the mere name sets up an inner obstacle that brings weariness before activity can even begin. The same thing happens with grammar. I once knew a very intelligent Italian girl who made spelling mistakes that were really incredible in anyone of her age and culture. All efforts to correct her were in vain, her mistakes seemed to increase, and even reading the classics did no good. But one day to my amazement I saw her write in correct and pure Italian. I cannot treat of her case here, but what is certain is that the correct form of expression existed, but an occult force tyrannically held it under, sending forth instead of shower of mistakes.

It may be asked which of the two forms of deviation, fugues or psychic barriers, is the most serious. In our normalising schools fugues like those we have quoted affecting imagination and play have been easiest to overcome. This may be illustrated by the following analogy. If someone flees from a place because he has not found there the things he needed or if a whole people flees in general exodus because a country does not provide the necessary food, we can always conceive of their being summoned back if conditions of environment are changed. We can cry to them: "Come back. We will provide better conditions for your lives. You will be able to use your energies in a pleasant environment."

In fact one of the things we have often noticed in our schools is the rapidity of transformation in disorderly and violent children, who seem in a flash to come back from a distant world. The change in them is not only the outwardly apparent transformation of disorder into work, but it lies deeper, and shows itself as serenity and content. The disappearance of their deviations comes about as a spontaneous event, a natural transformation, and yet had such deviation not been rectified in childhood, it would have remained throughout life. In fact, many adults who are considered richly endowed with imagination have really only vague feelings towards their environment and made contact only with sensory realities. They are those who are said to be temperamentally imaginative; they are untidy, and always ready to admire lights, the sky, colours, flowers, landscapes, music; they are sensible to things of life as to a novel. But they do not love the light they admire, they would be incapable of stopping to learn about it; the stars that inspire them could not hold their attention long enough for them to acquire the smallest knowledge of astronomy. They have artistic tendencies, but bring forth no artistic productions; for they are incapable of gaining any real technical proficiency. As a rule they do not know what to do with their hands. They cannot keep them still, nor use them. They touch things nervously and are liable to break them. They will distractedly tear to pieces the flower they so much admired. They cannot create anything beautiful, they cannot make their lives happy, they do not know how to find the real poetry of the world. They are lost, if no one saves them; for they mistake their organic weakness and incapacity for a higher state. Now the origin of this state, which predisposes them to real psychological diseases, lay at the roots of their lives, at the age when confusion was easiest and when a barred road led to deviations at first imperceptible.

Psychic inhibitions, on the other hand, are far harder to overcome, even in small children. They form an inner wall that shuts in the spirit, hiding it to defend it from the world. A secret drama is taking place behind those manifold barriers, which are often a defence against all that is beautiful outside and which would be a source of riches and happiness. Study, the secrets of science and mathematics, the fascinating refinements of an immortal tongue, music—all are henceforth the "enemy" from whom it is necessary to find isolation. This strange transformation of energy projects a darkness that covers and hides what should be an object of love and life. Studies were a weariness, and led to an aversion to the world instead of to a preparation to take part in it.

Barriers! This suggestive word by association of ideas reminds us of all the defences man set up about his body before a knowledge of physical hygiene showed him a healthier mode of living. Men defended themselves from sun, air, water, surrounding themselves with barriers, building walls through which no light could pass, keeping their windows shut night and day, while they were already too small to let through sufficient air, covering themselves with heavy clothing, layer upon layer, like the wrappings of an onion, which made the body reluctant to plunge itself into water, keeping the pores of their skin closed against the purifying air. The physical environment of man was barricaded against life.

From the social standpoint, too, we see phenomenon that remind us of barriers. Why do men isolate themselves one from the other, and why does every family group shut itself up with a feeling of isolation and of repugnance towards other groups? The family does not isolate itself to find enjoyment in itself, but to separate itself from others. These barriers are not built to defend love. The family barriers are closed, insurmountable, more powerful than the walls of the house. So too are the barriers separating classes and nations. National barriers are not put up to separate off a united and uniform group, so that it shall be free and secure from danger. Anxiety for isolation and defence reinforces the barriers between nation and nation, and hinders the circulation of individuals and of their produce. Why, if civilisation comes about through exchange? Are national barriers too a psychological phenomenon, due to some great suffering, the endurance of some extreme violence? Pain has organised itself, and has been so immense that ever stronger and thicker barriers have crippled the lives of nations.

## THE DEPENDENT CHILD

There are certain submissive children whose psychic energies are not strong enough to find a refuge in flight and escape from the influence of the adult, and who therefore attach themselves to an adult who tends to replace their activities by his own; such children become extremely dependent on the adult. The want of vital energy, though they are unconscious of it, sets them whining. These are the children who are always grumbling; they seem unhappy and pass for creatures with very delicate feelings and sensitive to affection. They are always bored without knowing it, and they have recourse to others, to grown-ups, because by themselves they are unable to throw off the depression of boredom. They attach themselves to someone, as though their vitality depended on others. They ask the grown-up to help them, to play with them, to tell them stories, sing to them, and beg him not to leave them. With such a child, the adult becomes a slave; a strange reciprocity holds both down, but the impression they give is one of great mutual understanding and intense affection. These are the children who are always asking why, with question after question, as though they hungered for knowledge. But if you observe them carefully you perceive that they have not listened to an answer before they have put another question. What appears as curiosity to know is really a means of binding the person whom they need to sustain them. They are ready to renounce their movements and obey every inhibiting command on the part of the adult, who finds it very easy to substitute his own will for that of the child, the child docilely giving way in everything. Thus there is a grave danger of the child's falling into apathy, that apathy that is called idleness and sloth. The adult welcomes such a state of things, because it does not impede his own activities, but it is really the extreme limit to which deviation can reach. What is sloth but a depression of the spiritual organism? It corresponds to the failing of physical strength in someone stricken with a grave illness; here it is the depression of the vital and creative psychological energies. The Christian religion recognises sloth among the seven deadly sins, that is, as bringing danger of death to the soul. The adult has driven the child's soul into itself, he has breathed over it his useless assistance, the substitution of his own activity, his suggestive power, and he has quenched it. And yet he perceives nothing.

## POSSESSIVENESS

In the very young child and in the normalized child there is an urge that leads them towards forces in order to act with them. This outward movement towards their environment is not something cold, but a penetrating love, a vital sign comparable to hunger. In a hungry person there is an urge to seek food. It is not associated with logical reasoning. He does not say: "It is a long time since I last ate; without eating I cannot maintain my strength or live; it is therefore necessary that I should look for nourishing substances and eat them." Hunger is a discomfort that brings an irresistible urge towards food. And the child has a kind of hunger that carries him towards his surroundings, to seek for things that can feed his spirit, nourishing himself by activity. "As children newly born, let us love spiritual milk." In this impulse, that is, in love of his environment, lies the basic characteristic of man. It would not be correct to say that the child has a passion for his environment, for passion implies something impulsive and transitory; it implies the urge to a "vital episode". The impetus provided by a child's love of his environment leads him instead to a constant activity, a continual fire, like the continual burning of the elements of the body in contact with oxygen, giving the gentle heat natural to the living body. The active child expresses himself as a creature that lives in an environment suitable to his needs, where he finds the means without which he cannot fulfil himself.

If the child is denied this environment of psychic life, everything in him is weakened, deviated and shut away. He becomes an impenetrable, enigmatic being, empty, incapable, naughty, bored, cut off from society.

Now if it is rendered impossible for the child to find the motives of activity that would develop him, he sees only "things", and wants *to possess* them. To take, to possess, here is something easy, where intellectual light and love are useless. Energy bursts forth in another direction. "I want," says the child, seeing a gold watch on which he cannot tell the time. "No, me!" cries another, ready to break it and therefore to render it useless, as long as he can take possession of it. And thus begin competition between persons and destructive struggles over things.

Almost all moral deviations are consequences of this first step that decides between love and possession, and which may set the child on one of two diverging paths, carrying him forward with the full force of life. The active part of the child projects itself outward like the tentacles of an octopus, to crush and destroy things he passionately clasps. Feelings of ownership make him vehemently attached to things and ready to defend them as he would defend himself.

Sturdier, active children defend their things even by fighting against other children who feel a like desire to possess them. They are continually quarrelling, because they want the same thing or because they want something another has. Here is the origin of reactions anything but loving, of an explosion of feelings anything but fraternal, leading to struggle and war about trifles, something of no importance whatever. But it is not really of no importance, but very grave. There has been a displacement, a darkening of something that should have existed, an energy has been deviated. It is thus an inner evil and not the outer thing in itself that causes possessiveness.

As everyone knows, attempts are made to give a kind of moral training by means of exhortations, in order that the child should not become thus attached to external things. The foundation of such teaching is respect for the property of others. But when the child has reached this point, he has already crossed the bridge by which man has separated himself from the grandeur of his inner life, and that is why he turns with desire to outward things. The germ has filtered into the child soul so deeply that such characteristics are judged proper to human nature.

Even children of submissive character turn their interest to outward material things of no value. Such children, however, have a different way of "possessing" which is not quarrelsome and as a rule does not lead them to competitive struggles. They tend rather to accumulate and hide things, so that people believe them natural collectors. But it is very different from collecting and classifying things under the guidance of a certain knowledge. We are speaking, instead, of children who accumulate the most varied and unrelated objects, which in themselves offer no attraction. Pathology recognizes cases of an empty and illogical collecting that is a sign of mania, that is, dictated by a psychological anomaly, and this is to be found not only in mentally diseased adults, but also in delinquent children whose pockets are often crammed with useless and ill-assorted objects. There is a likeness between this and the collectionism of children of weak, submissive character, which is generally looked upon as quite normal. If someone takes away the things they have accumulated, such children seek to defend themselves as far as they are able. Adler, the psychologist, has given an interesting interpretation of such symptoms. He compares them to avarice, to the phenomenon to be found in the adult of which the germ can be recognized in infancy. It is the phenomenon through which a man is attached to many things and does not want to give them up even if they are of no use to him, a poisonous plant which has grown up as a result of a fundamental lack of balance.

Parents are pleased when their children defend their property; in this they see human nature and recognize a link with social life. Even the children who hoard and accumulate are human figures comprehensible in society.

## THE POWER CRAVING

Another characteristic deviation associated with possession is the desire for power. There is a power instinctive in man as the destined master of his environment, which leads him through love of that environment to possess himself of the outer world. But it is a deviation when power, instead of being a fruit of conquest, building up human personality, is directed to seizing and snatching at *things*.

Now the deviated child is confronted with an adult, who is for him a supremely powerful being with all things at his disposal. The child understands that his own power would be great indeed if he could act through the adult. Thus he begins to exploit the adult to obtain from him what he could never obtain in his own sphere. This process is perfectly understandable. It shows itself inevitably in all children, so much so that it is considered one of the commonest facts and one of those hardest to correct. It provides the typical example of child wilfulness; for it is logical and natural that a weak, incapable, imprisoned creature, once he has made the wonderful discovery that he can persuade a powerful, free being to procure advantages for him, should seek to obtain such advantages. The child makes the trial and begins to want things, and to want things over and above what the adult considers logically right for him, for his wants are boundless. The child is full of fancies, and the adult seems to be an omnipotent being, who can fulfil the desires of his dreams in all their dazzling splendour. Such a feeling finds full realisation in fairy stories, which may often appear as romances of the child soul. In fairy stories children feel their obscure wishes exalted in attractive guise. Whoever asks the fairies can obtain favours, riches far beyond any human power. There are good and bad fairies, beautiful and ugly ones. They may appear in the guise of poor people or rich people. Some live in the woods, some in enchanted palaces. They seem indeed the idealised projection of the child who lives among adults. There are old fairies like grandmothers and beautiful ones like mothers. There are fairies clad in rags, and fairies clad in gold, just as there are poor mothers and rich mothers with wonderful evening dresses, and all spoil their children. The adult, be he wretched or proud, is always a powerful being to the child, and thus in real life the child begins that attempt at exploitation that must end in conflict. In the beginning such a struggle is sweet; for the adult allows himself to be vanquished and gives way for the pleasure of seeing his child happy and contented. Yes, the adult who will prevent the child from washing his own hands will certainly try to satisfy his mania for possession. But the child, after a first victory, seeks a second, and the more the grown-up gives in, the more the child wants, till the illusion that the grown-up was made to see his child satisfied ends in bitter disappointment. Since the material world has inexorable limits, whereas imagination may wander in infinity, the moment comes when there is a real clash, a violent conflict. The child's wilfulness becomes the adult's punishment. Indeed, he at once recognises his fault and says, "I have spoilt my child."

Even the submissive child can vanquish the adult, by his affectionate ways, his tears, his pleading, his sad little face, his attractive graces. To him, too, the adult must give in, till he can give in no longer, and then comes the unhappiness that no deviation from a normal state can fail to bring. The adult reflects and at last realises that he has treated the child in such a way as to develop vices; then he tries to turn back and to correct him.

But everyone knows that nothing will correct a child's wilfulness. Neither exhortations nor punishments will be any good; it is as if you were to preach a long sermon to a man delirious with fever, telling him that it would be much better for him to be well and threatening to beat him if he does not make his temperature fall. The fact is that the adult spoiled his child not by giving way to him, but by preventing him from really living, thus driving him into a deviation of his natural development.

### THE INFERIORITY COMPLEX

The adult shows the child a *contempt* which consciously he is far from feeling; for he believes his child to be beautiful and perfect and projects into him his own pride and his own hope for the future. But there is a secret urge in him that is not merely the conviction that the child is "empty" or "naughty" and therefore to be filled and amended by himself; it is real though unacknowledged contempt for the child. The weak creature with which he is confronted is his own child. Where that child is concerned the adult is all-powerful. He has even the right to show feelings that he would be ashamed to show in the society of other adults. Among his obscure tendencies are avarice and a feeling of tyranny and absolutism. And thus in the home, camouflaged as paternal authority, the slow, continuous demolition of the child ego is brought about. If, for example, a grown-up sees the child moving a glass, he thinks and fears that the glass will get broken. At that moment avarice makes him look upon the glass as a treasure and in order to save it he will stop the child from moving. Perhaps the adult in question is a very rich man, who thinks he will increase his wealth tenfold so that his son may be even richer than he. But at that moment he feels that the glass is immensely precious, to be saved at any cost. On the other hand, he thinks: "Why should this child put the glass in one way when I have put it in another? Am I not the authority who can dispose of things as he likes?" And yet this adult in his heart would be content to make any sacrifice for his child. He dreams of seeing him one day triumphant; he would like him to become a famous, powerful man. But at that moment the tyrannical, authoritarian tendency surges up in him, frittering itself away in defence of an object of no value. In fact, if a servant made the same movement, the father would smile, and if a guest happened to break the glass he would hasten to reassure him that it did not matter, that the glass was of no value. The child must thus notice with despairing constancy that he alone is considered dangerous to things, and thus he alone is thought incapable of touching them; he is an inferior creature worth almost less than things.

There is another complexus of ideas to be considered in relation to the inner building-up of the child. He needs not only to touch things and to work with them, but to follow a sequence of actions to its completion, and this is of the greatest importance in the inward building-up of his personality. The adult no longer consciously notes the sequence of his daily actions, for he possesses them as something that is part of his very existence, as a mode of being. When he gets up in the morning, he knows that he must do this and that, and he does them as the most natural things in the world. The sequence of actions has become almost automatic, and he no longer notices it any more than he notices his breathing or his heart-beats. The child on the contrary needs to lay this foundation. But he can never make a plan of action to be carried out consecutively. If he is playing, a grown-up comes to say it is time to go for a walk, and dresses him and takes him away. Or else, when he is performing some little task, such as filling a bucket with pebbles, one of his mother's friends comes along, and his mother calls him away from his work to show him to the new arrival. In the child's life grown-ups are continually intervening, powerful beings able to dispose of his life without ever consulting him, without considering him, showing that his actions have no value; whereas in his presence, an adult will not turn to another, not even to a servant, to interrupt what he is doing without saying, "Will you be so kind," or "If you can." The child therefore feels that he is a creature different from all others, with a special inferiority that sets him below all others. Now, as we have said, a sequence of actions resulting from an inwardly predetermined plan is of the very highest importance in the child's development. One day the adult will explain to him that he must be responsible for his own actions, but the first foundation of such responsibility lies in a complete pattern of the connection between one action and another, and in a judgment as to their significance. But the child feels only that all his actions are considered insignificant. The adult, the parent, who complains that he cannot arouse that feeling of responsibility and mastery over his own actions in his son, himself step by step broke down the child's conception of the continuity of the successive actions of life, and his feeling of his own dignity. In such cases, instead of feeling a consciousness of his own dignity, the child bears within him an obscure conviction of inferiority and impotence. To assume any responsibility implies a conviction of being master of one's own actions and confidence in oneself. There is no discouragement like that which springs from the conviction, "I can't." If a paralysed child were told to race with a very quick one, he would not wish to run at all; if a skilful giant were set to box with a small, inexpert man, the latter would not wish to fight. The possibility of effort is quenched before it has been tried, leaving behind a feeling of incapacity before the test has been made. Now the adult is continually quenching the child's sense of effort, when he humiliates the child's sense of his own strength and convinces him of incapacity; for, in fact, the adult does not content himself with impeding the child in his actions, but tells him: "You *can't* do that, it is no use trying," or if it is someone of rougher manners, it will be, "You silly, why d'you want to do that, don't you see you can't?" And this offends not only the child's work and his sequences of actions, but his very personality. It implants in his soul the feeling not only that his actions have no value, but that his personality itself is inept and incapable. Then comes discouragement, lack of self-confidence, for if we find that it is someone stronger who prevents us from doing something we had intended, we can say to ourselves that his place may be taken by someone weaker, and then we can begin again. But if the adult convinces the child that the incapacity lies in himself, then a land of cloud covers his mind, bringing timidity, and a kind of apathy and a fear, which become constitutional. All these feelings together form the *inner obstacle* that psycho-analysis describes as an "inferiority complex." It is an obstacle that may remain permanently as a humiliating sense of incapacity and inferiority to others, and this prevents participation in the social tests that arise at every step of life.

This inferiority complex leads to timidity, hesitancy in decision, sudden withdrawals before any difficulty or criticism with an outward expression of despair in the ready tears that accompany such painful situations.

Now the child's normal nature reveals as one of its most striking characteristics self-confidence and surety of action. While the little boy at San Lorenzo showed the disappointed visitors that though it was a holiday the children could open the workroom and work even in the absence of their teacher, he showed a perfect and balanced strength of character, which was not a presuming on his own strength but a knowledge and control of it. The child knows what he is undertaking and dominates the sequence of actions necessary to its performance so that he is able to do it with absolute simplicity without feeling he has done anything out of the ordinary. In the same way a child who was putting words together out of a movable alphabet, showed no perturbation when the Queen of Italy stopped in front of him and told him to make *"Viva l'Itafia!"* He at once began to put the letters back in their order, as calmly as if he had been alone. In homage to the Queen, one might have expected that he would have suspended what he was doing, in order to do what she had asked of him. But there was a special detail not to be overlooked: he had to put all the letters back in their order before using them again for other words. And, in fact, having done so, he set to work to compose the words *"Viva l'Italia!"* Here was someone able to dominate his emotions and his actions, a little man four years old, who could orient him self with perfect surety to meet the incidents that arose in his environment.

## FEAR

Another form of deviation is fear, which is considered a natural characteristic of childhood. When people speak of a fearful child they refer to a fear resulting from some deep-seated disturbance, almost independently of the conditions of his environment, and which, like shyness, is a part of his character. There are submissive children who, one might say, are enveloped as with an anguished aura of fear. Others, on the contrary, who are sturdy and active and courageous in danger, may reveal mysterious and illogical fears that cannot be overcome. These states of mind may be interpreted as resulting from strong impressions received in the past, as, for instance, fear of crossing a road, fear that there are cats under the bed, fear at the sight of a hen, that is to say, states similar to the phobias psychiatry has studied in the adult. All these forms of fear exist in an especial manner in the children who are "dependent on the adult," and the adult, in order to obtain obedience, profits by the nebulous state of consciousness of the child, to impress upon it artificially fear of vague beings who work in darkness. This is one of the most pernicious forms of the adult's defence against the child; it aggravates his natural fear of darkness and peoples it with terrifying images.

Everything that brings the child into contact with reality and allows him to gain experience of the things of his environment, and hence an understanding of such things, tends to liberate him from the disturbing state of fear; In our normalizing schools the disappearance of subconscious fears, or their failure to appear, is one of the clearest results. An important Spanish writer wished to write of this phenomenon which struck him as a fact worthy to be known by the public. He had three daughters, who were already big girls, and a fourth little girl, who attended one of our schools. If there was a thunderstorm during the night the youngest was the only one of the four who was not afraid, and she would lead her elder sisters through the house to their parents' room, where they used to take refuge on such occasions. Her presence, through her freedom from mysterious fears, was a real comfort to the others. And thus if, as sometimes happened, the bigger girls were afraid at night, they used to go to their little sister in order to throw off the impression.

A "state of fear" is different from fear arising from a normal instinct of self-preservation in the presence of danger. Now this kind of normal fear is less frequent among children than among grown-ups. This is not only because children have had less experience than adults of outward dangers. One might even say that it is a prevailing characteristic of childhood to face danger, and that this is proportionately far more developed than in adults. In fact, children repeatedly expose themselves to danger, like the children in the streets who hang on to moving traffic or in the country climb the highest trees or crawl down precipices. They will fling themselves into the sea or into rivers, and often learn to swim at their own risk. There is no counting the number of cases of child heroism when children have saved or tried to save the lives of their playfellows. I will quote only the case of a fire in an institution in California, in which one wing was reserved for blind children. The bodies of normal children were found, who, though living in another part of the building, had run to lead the blind ones to safety. In child organisations like the Boy Scouts every day brings some example of heroism.

It may be asked whether normalization develops this heroic tendency to be found so frequently among children. In our experience of normalization we have had no heroic episodes, unless we accept the expression of some noble desire, which is, however, a very different thing from a real heroic action. (There was the child of five who on hearing of the Messina earthquake wrote a sentence for the first time, "If I was big I would go and help.") But the real and ordinary incidents in the lives of our children are to be referred to a "prudence" that allows them to avoid dangers and hence to live among them. For example, they are early able to handle knives at table or even in the kitchen, to handle matches and to light the fire or candles. They can be left free near ponds or cisterns, and can cross the road in town. In short, they are able to control their actions and at the same time control their rasher impulses, thus attaining a serene and loftier form of life. Normalization therefore does not make them run into danger but develops a prudence that allows them to go about in the midst of dangers, knowing them and mastering them.

## LYING

Psychic deviation, though it may show an infinity of particular characteristics, like the buds and branches of a flourishing tree, springs always from the same deep roots, and it is in dealing with these that the single secret of normalization lies, whereas in ordinary psychology and in current methods of education such particular consequences are considered separate defects to be studied and dealt with separately as though they were actually independent of each other.

One of the chief of such particular consequences is lying. Lies are like clothing that hides the soul—a whole trousseau of many different garments; for there are so many and such different kinds of lies, each with a different significance. There are "normal lies" and pathological lies. The old psychiatry dealt extensively with the irrepressible lying associated with hysteria, when the lie covers the whole soul and language becomes a fabric of lies. It was also psychiatry that drew attention to the lies told by children in children's courts, and in general to the possible unconscious lying of children called as witnesses. It was startling to realise or discover that the child whose "innocent soul" was almost a synonym of truth (truth speaking through the mouth of innocence), might bear false witness in all sincerity. The attention of criminological psychologists was drawn to these amazing facts and it was recognised that such children were truly sincere and that their lies were due to a form of mental confusion aggravated by the emotion of the moment.

This substitution of falsehood for truth, whether as a permanent state or as an episodic event, is certainly something far removed from the normal fibs of a child seeking to hide himself by conscious self-defence. But in normal children arid in ordinary daily life we also find lies that have nothing to do with defence. The lie may be a real invention, born of a need to recount something fantastic, with the added piquant pleasure of having it believed as true by others; yet it is not told in order to deceive or with any aim of personal advantage. It is then a genuine form of art, like that of an actor who identifies himself with the character he plays. I will give an example: One day some children told me that their mother, when someone important was coming to dinner, "prepared some vegetable juices full of vitamins with her own hands, as an advertisement for eating things raw. She succeeded, they said, in making such a delicious natural juice that her guest said he would use it and tell others of it. The story was so detailed and so interesting that I asked their mother to tell me how she prepared her vitamin juices. She replied that she had never even thought of making anything of the kind. Here is an example of something wholly created by a child's imagination, translated into a full-fledged lie and produced in society, with no other aim than the pure pleasure of romancing.

Lies of this kind are almost the opposite of others which are told from laziness, when the child will not bother to think what was the truth. Sometimes, however, a lie may be the result of astute reasoning. I once knew a little boy of six, who had been temporarily sent to boarding-school. The teacher in charge of the group of children in which he found himself was particularly suited to her office and had a great admiration for this particular child. After a time the little boy complained to his mother of this teacher, giving a quantity of details against her. He described her as altogether too severe. His mother went to the headmistress to make enquiries, and received full proof that the teacher in question had a real weakness for her son and had always surrounded him with affectionate care. The mother then confronted him and asked him why he had told such lies. "They weren't lies," he said, "but I couldn't say it was the headmistress who was nasty." It did not seem as if he lacked the courage to accuse the headmistress, but rather as if he felt the force of convention. Much could be said of the cunning of which children are capable in adapting themselves to their environment.

Weak-charactered, submissive children, on the contrary, tell lies that are made up on the spur of the moment, as by a defensive reflex, without a mentally elaborated content. These are the naive, unorganised, improvised and therefore easily recognisable lies against which parents and teachers wage war, forgetting that their significance is clearly and genuinely a defence against the attacks of the adult. The charges which the adult in such cases makes against the child, accusing him of weakness and shameful inferiority and denouncing the unworthiness of such lies, are a simple recognition that such lies reveal an inferior being.

Fibbing is one of the psychological phenomena concerning the intelligence which in infancy are still in process of formation but which organise themselves with time and come to form so important a part of human social life as to be indispensable, decent and even aesthetic, like clothes for the body.

In our normalizing schools the child's soul sheds the camouflage of conventionalism and reveals its natural sincerity. None the less, fibbing is not one of the deviations that vanish as if by a miracle. It requires a reconstruction rather than a conversion. Clarity of ideas, union with reality, freedom of spirit and an active interest in lofty objects form an environment propitious to the reconstruction of a sincere soul.

But if we analyse social life, we find that it is permeated by lying as by an atmosphere that could not be dissipated without convulsing society. In fact, many of our children who went on to ordinary secondary schools were judged impertinent or insubordinate simply because they were much more sincere than others, and had not developed certain necessary forms of adaptation. This their teachers did not recognise. Discipline and social relations were indeed organised on lies, and an unfamiliar sincerity seemed to upset the moral construction established as the basis of education.

One of the most brilliant contributions of psychoanalysis to the story of the human soul is its interpretation of camouflage as subconscious adaptation. It is the adult's forms of camouflage and not the child's fibs that represent the terrible garment that comes to form part of life, to be compared to the pelt or plumage of the animal kingdom; that is, to a protective clothing that covers, embellishes and defends the vital machinery at work beneath it. Camouflage is the lie of feeling, a lie that man builds in himself in order to live, or better, in order to survive, in a world with which his pure and natural feelings would be in conflict. And since it is not possible to live in a state of perpetual conflict, the soul must adapt itself. One of the most singular of such forms of camouflage is the attitude of the adult to the child. The adult sacrifices the child's needs to his own, but he does not lie in a state—which would be intolerable—of recognising that he does so. So he persuades himself that he is exercising a natural right and is acting for the child's future good. When the little one defends itself, the soul of the adult is not awakened to the true state of things, but all that the child does in defence of his life is called disobedience, or bad tendencies. Little by little the voice of truth and justice, faint as it was, disappears, and its place is taken by brilliant, solid, permanent forms of camouflage which appear as duty, right, authority, prudence, etc. "The heart hardens, it turns to ice and shines like something transparent. All that falls against it is broken.... My heart has become a stone, I strike it and it is my hand that is wounded."[1] It is by a beautiful metaphor that in the depths of Dante's Inferno, where all love is extinguished, and only hatred remains, there is ice. Love and hate are two differing states of the soul, like the liquid and solid states of water. Yes, such camouflage is the lie of the spirit, which helps man to adapt himself to the organised deviations of society, and which little by little hardens what was once love into forms of hate.

This is the fearful lie that hides in the secret depths of the subconscious soul.

## REPERCUSSIONS ON PHYSICAL LIFE

There are a large number of characteristics which psychic deviations bring in their train, some of which appear of a wholly different order, for they affect the functioning of the body. Today the psychological causes of many physical disturbances form a chapter of medicine that has received considerable study. There are also defects that seem essentially bodily of which the remote origins lie in the domain of the mind. Some of these, such as digestive disturbances, affect children especially. Sturdy, active children show tendencies to a kind of voracious hunger which it is hard to check by training or diet. Such children eat more than is necessary through an irresistible urge that is often complacently considered a "good appetite," though it leads to digestive disturbances and toxic conditions which bring them continually into the doctor's hands.

---

[1] "Da Francesca a Beatrice," by Victoria Ocampo.

Already in older days a vice of a moral order was recognized in the wild tendency of the body to absorb more food than it needed, doing itself no good, or rather doing itself harm. Such a tendency seems to reveal a suspension of the normal sensibility towards food, which should not only urge to the quest of food, but also limit its consumption to what is necessary. This is what we find in the animals, the health of which is entrusted to a guiding instinct of preservation. The instinct of preservation has two aspects, the one related to the environment, the avoidance of dangers, the other to the individual itself, and governing its consumption of food. In animals the prevailing instinct not only leads them to proper food but determines its quantity. It is indeed one of the most distinctive characteristics of all animal species. Whether they eat much or little; each species in a natural state observes the measure nature has implanted in it in the form of instinct.

Man, on the other hand, shows a gluttony, which not only leads him to a senseless accumulation of excessive quantities of food but brings a tendency to consume substances that are actually poisonous. We may say then that the appearance of psychic deviations brings with it the loss of the protective sensibilities that would guide man towards health. Of this we find clear proof in the "deviated" child, who at once shows a lack of balance in his feeding. Food allures him from without by its appearance, it is greeted only by the external sense of taste, but the inner vital factor, the preserving sensibility, is enfeebled or lost. One of the most startling demonstrations in our normalizing schools was the fact that the children, as they recovered from psychic deviations and were restored to a normal state, lost all signs of greediness and ceased to show their former voracious hunger. What interested them was the precise performance of each action, so that they might eat with correct gestures. This restoration of vital sensibility aroused an almost incredulous wonder in the early days, when people spoke of child conversions. Certain scenes of child life formed the subject of minute description, in order to convince people that this phenomenon was a real fact. Tiny children, when the hour came for a well-deserved meal and they were faced by an appetising dish, spent their time adjusting their napkins, looking at the covers so as to remember the exact way of holding and using each implement, or of helping a smaller comrade, and sometimes they were so meticulous that the dish got cold before they ate it. Other children were sad because they had hoped to be chosen to wait at table, and instead there they were condemned to the easiest task of all, that of eating.

A counter-proof of the correspondence between psychological factors and food is to be found in an opposite fact. Submissive children have a strange and often invincible reluctance to eat at all. Many people have experienced this difficulty in feeding certain children. They refuse to eat, to such an extent as to create real difficulties in the family or in educational institutions. Such a phenomenon is more striking when it occurs in institutions for poor, weak children, whom one would expect to seize any favourable occasion for eating their fill. It may become so serious as to produce a physical decline impervious to all attempts at cure. This refusal of food must not be confused with dyspepsia, when the digestive organs are in a genuinely abnormal state, producing lack of appetite. Here the child is prevented from eating by some psychological cause. In some cases it springs from a defensive impulse against attempts to feed him, or when the child is forced to eat quickly, that is, with the rhythm of the adult. The child has a rhythm of his own, and this has now been recognised by child specialists, who note that children do not eat all the food they need at one go, but interpose long pauses in their slow eating. This we find already in babies before they are weaned. They stop sucking not because they have had enough, but in order to rest, for their rhythm is not only slow but intermittent. We can therefore recognise a possible defensive impulse, like a barrier, against the violence by which the baby was forced to feed independently of the laws of its nature. There are, however, cases in which there can be no question of such defence. A child may seem almost constitutionally lacking in appetite. He is incurably pale, and no treatment, not even open-air life, sunlight, or sea air can mend him. But in such cases we find that he is overshadowed by some adult to whom he is extremely attached, and who exercises a repressive influence. Then only one thing can cure him—to send him away from such influence to an environment where he will be psychologically free and active, so that he will lose an attachment that is deforming his spirit.

In support of our thesis we may note that there has always been a recognition of the relationship between psychological life and those physical phenomena that are considered most remote from mind, such as eating. Gluttony indeed is classed among the vices that "darken the mind." It is interesting to see the precision with which St. Thomas Aquinas underlines the connection between gluttony and intellectual conditions. He maintains that gluttony blunts judgment and as a result weakens man's cognition of intelligible realities. In the child, however, we find the reverse process at work; psychological disturbance giving rise to gluttony. The Christian religion so relates this vice to disturbances of a spiritual order that it puts it among the seven deadly sins, that is, among those that lead to the death of the soul, to a way that is barred through a transgression of some of the mysterious laws that govern the universe. At the same time, from another, wholly modern and scientific, standpoint, psycho-analysis indirectly supports our theory of a loss of the guiding instinct or preserving sensibility. To this, however, psycho-analysis gives a different interpretation, and speaks of the "death-instinct." That is to say, it recognises in man a natural tendency to assist the inevitable advent of death, facilitating it and hastening it, and even running to meet it by suicide. Man becomes attached to poisons like alcohol, opium, cocaine, by an irresistible urge, that is, he attaches himself to death and summons it, instead of attaching himself to life and salvation. But does not all this indicate precisely the loss of a vital inner sensibility, which should work for the preservation of the individual? If such a tendency were due to the inevitability of death, it should exist in all creatures. We should rather say that all psychic deviation sets man on the road to death and makes him active in destroying his own life, and that this terrible tendency already shows itself in a faint and almost imperceptible form in early infancy.

All illness may have a psychological coefficient, for psychological life and physical life are closely connected, but abnormality in feeding opens the door to all and summons all. Sometimes, however, the illness is merely a semblance, with purely psychological causes, as though it were an image and not a reality. Psycho-analysis has thrown much light on such cases in dealing with organic neurosis, a flight into illness. Organic neuroses are not simulated illnesses, but present genuine symptoms, feverish temperatures, and true functional disturbances that sometimes appear serious. And yet such illnesses are not physical, for they are generated in the subconscious by psychological factors able to dominate physiological laws. By illness the ego is able to escape from unpleasant situations and obligations. The illness resists all treatment, and disappears only when the ego is freed from the conditions it sought to escape. I witnessed cases of this kind in a religious educational institution for little girls, which from the point of view of hygiene left nothing to be desired. And yet there were sick children in the infirmary, some of them with persistent temperatures that it was not easy to cure. These illnesses disappeared with the abolition of the obligation of attendance at the first early morning Mass.

Many illnesses and morbid states, like many moral defects, may disappear when children are placed in a free environment and allowed to engage in normalising activities. Today, many child-specialists recognise our schools as houses of health where they may send children with functional diseases which have resisted all ordinary attempts at cure. Surprising cures have been thus obtained.

# PART III

# The Child and Society

# 10

## Homo Laborans

### THE CONFLICT BETWEEN CHILD AND ADULT

The conflict between adult and child is the starting point for consequences that will widen and widen almost to infinity in the life of man, like the ripples that spread out further and further if you drop a stone on the clear surface of quiet waters. Such consequences are vibrations that spread out in a circle on every side.

This is precisely what medicine and psycho-analysis have discovered in going back to the original causes of physical and mental diseases. Psycho-analysts must travel a long road in their search for the primary origins of mental diseases, like the explorers, who, seeking the sources of the Nile, had far to go, meeting terrifying cataracts on their journey, till they reached the calm waters of the great lakes. Those sciences that have sought to sound the origins of weakness, incapacity, resistance and distortion in the human soul, have had to go far beyond immediate causes, far deeper than conscious and comprehensible causes, till they reached the quiet waters, the body and soul of the young child.

But if we want to take the contrary path and are interested in the new history of humanity as it is written in the secrecy of the formation of its elements, then we can start from the calm lakes of first infancy and follow the tumultuous river of life as it springs forth and flows down from the mountains, in and out of obstacles, deviating and twisting in its difficult journey, leaping down abysses, able to do anything but remain still, anything but cease to follow the course of the turbulent mass of its waters.

If the most visible ills afflicting adult man, physical disease and nervous and mental disease, can really be traced to childhood, it is the life of the child that can show us the first symptoms.

There is, however, another fact to be considered, and that is that every great and visible evil is surrounded by an infinity of lesser evils. The cases of death through disease are few compared to the cases in which the same disease is cured. And if illness is the cause of a weakness that has not been able to resist its assault, there must be many who are weak even if they have not remained a prey to disease. Abnormal conditions predisposing to disease can be compared to the waves that transmit the vibrations of the ether to infinity. That is why anyone examining water to know if it is pure and fit for drinking does not take it all but examines a small quantity of it only. If that portion is infected, he concludes that all the water is infected. Thus if there are deaths from disease or men lost in mental or psychic confusion, we must say that there is error in the whole of mankind.

This is no new idea. Already in the days of Moses it was recognised that there was an error at the very origin of mankind, an original sin indicating that all mankind was infected and lost. Original sin seems an illogical and unjust conception because it envisages the possible condemnation of the innumerable innocents destined to make up humanity, but we may observe a parallel fact, for we find innocent children condemned to bear the fatal consequences of a development distorted by mistakes repeated through the ages. The causes of which we treat lie in the conflict that exists at the base of human life, a conflict big with consequences and which has not been sufficiently explored.

## THE INSTINCT TO WORK

Before these revelations of true child nature, the laws governing the building up of psychological life had remained absolutely unknown. The study of the sensitive periods as directing the formation of man may become one of the sciences of the greatest practical use to mankind.

The foundation of development and growth lies in progressive and ever more intimate relations between the individual and his environment; for the development of individuality, and of what is called the freedom of the child, can be nothing else than his progressive independence of the adult, realised by means of a suitable environment in which he can find the necessary means of evolving his functions. This is as clear and simple as the fact that in weaning a baby we prepare baby food from cereals, fruit juices and vegetables, that is to say, by using the products of the outer world in place of the mother's milk.

The mistake in envisaging the freedom of the child in education has lain in imagining his hypothetical independence of the adult without corresponding preparation of the environment. This preparation of the environment is part of the science of education, just as the preparation of baby food is part of the science of health. Now the preparation of the psychic environment, in its essential principles, as a basis of a new education, has been outlined by the child himself clearly enough for it to become a practical reality.

Among the revelations the child has brought us, there is one of fundamental importance, the phenomenon of normalisation through work. Thousands and thousands of experiences among children of every race enable us to state that this phenomenon is the most certain datum verified in psychology or education. It is certain that the child's attitude towards work represents a vital instinct; for without work his personality cannot organise itself and deviates from the normal lines of its construction. Man builds himself through working. Nothing can take the place of work, neither physical well-being nor affection, and, on the other hand, deviations cannot be corrected by either punishment or example. Man builds himself through working, working with his hands, but using his hands as the instruments of his ego, the organ of his individual mind and will, which shapes its own existence face to face with its environment. The child's instinct confirms the fact that work is an inherent tendency in human nature; it is the characteristic instinct of the human race.

How then could it ever have come to pass that work, which should represent the supreme satisfaction, the centre of health and regeneration, as it does for the child, should be rejected by the adult man? However could it have been thought that work was a product of harsh necessities created by his environment? Perhaps because work in human society rests on mistaken foundations. It develops from deviated man, deviated through possession, power, apathy, attachment, so that the deep-seated instinct remains hidden as a suppressed characteristic. Then work depends only on external circumstances, or on struggles between deviated men. It becomes forced labour, giving rise to potent psychic barriers, and thus becomes hard and repellent.

But when through exceptional circumstances work is the result of an inner, instinctive impulse, then even in the adult it assumes a wholly different character. Such work is fascinating, irresistible, and it raises man above deviations and inner conflicts. Such is the work of the inventor or discoverer, the heroic efforts of the explorer, or the compositions of the artist, that is to say, the work of men gifted with such an extraordinary power as to enable them to rediscover the instinct of their species in the patterns of their own individuality. This instinct is then a fountain that bursts through the hard outer crust and rises, through a profound urge, to fall, as refreshing rain, on arid humanity. It is through this urge that the true progress of civilisation takes place.

## THE CHARACTERISTICS OF THE TWO KINDS OF WORK

The adult and the child, made to love one another and to live together, find themselves in conflict through an incomprehension that corrodes the roots of life, and which takes place in impenetrable secrecy.

The questions bearing on this conflict are manifold and some, which are clear and tangible, affect outward social relations. The adult has a mission to fulfil which has been so complicated and intensified that he finds it ever harder to suspend it as he must do if he is to follow the child, adapting himself to the child's rhythm and the psychological needs of his growth. But on the other hand, the increasing complexity and speed of the adult's environment becomes more and more unsuited to the child. We can imagine a simple and peaceful state of primitive life in which the little child finds a natural refuge. He sees the adult doing simple work in slow rhythm, he is surrounded by domestic animals and sees them living round him. He touches things and tries to work without arousing any protest. He sleeps when he is sleepy, throwing himself down in the shade of a tree. But little by little civilisation closes the social world to the child. Everything is over-regulated, too narrow, too encumbered, too fast. Not only is the quick rhythm of the busy adult an obstacle to him, but the machine comes along, carrying away like an impetuous wind every little vestige of the world in which the child could take refuge. Then he cannot live actively. Care of him implies saving his life from the dangers that multiply about him in the outer world. Thus he becomes a refugee, a helpless creature, a slave. No one thinks of the need of creating a special environment for his life, no one thinks that he too needs to be active and to work. It is necessary to realise that there are two social questions because there are two forms of life, and hence two needs to consider—the social question of the adult and the social question of the child. In each sphere there is essential work to be done; the work of the adult and the work of the child are both essential for the life of humanity.

## THE ADULT'S TASK

It is the adult's task to build an environment superimposed on nature, an outward work calling for activity and intelligent effort; it is what we call productive work, and is by its nature social, collective and organised. To attain the end of his work in society, man must necessarily order it, regulate it by norms that are the laws of society. They impose a collective discipline to which men voluntarily submit, for they themselves have recognised such laws as essential if social life is to be orderly and fruitful. But besides the laws which, representing local and temporal necessities, differ from one human group to another and from age to age, there are other basic laws of which the roots lie in human nature itself, and which concern work in itself; such laws are common to all men and all ages. One of these, the law of division of labour, universal in application among all living creatures, is necessary in order that men's production should be differentiated. Another natural law concerns, instead, the individual worker and is the law of least effort by which man seeks to produce the most he can, working as little as he can. This law is of very great importance not because of the existence of the wish to work as little as possible but because, by following it, production is increased with less expenditure of energy. This is a principle of such practical utility that it applies also to the machine taking the place of human labour or completing it.

There are the social and natural "good laws" of adaptation in work.

But not everything proceeds in accordance with these "good laws," for the material with which man works and produces wealth is limited, and, in the competitive struggle that ensues, the application of such laws degenerates.

Then evil human habits come to the fore, and seizure of others' labour takes the place of division of labour. In place of the law of least effort the principle of making others work creeps in: "Let them work so that I may profit by their labour while I rest." Such degenerations combine with the "good laws" and establish the social form of adult labour, under a camouflage of the right of property.

The child, who is essentially a natural being, lives with the adult as far as his material existence is concerned. But he remains permanently alien to the social labour of the adult; his activity cannot be used in social production. We must indeed hold this principle present to our consciousness that the child has no possibility of sharing in the social labour of the adult. If we take as symbol of manual work that of the smith striking with the sledge on the anvil, the child cannot make such an effort. If we take as symbol of intellectual work that of the scientist as he handles his instruments in some difficult piece of research, the child cannot make the smallest contribution in this field. Or if we think of a legislator meditating on the best laws, his place can never be taken by the child.

The child is thus essentially alien to this society of men and might express his position in the words of the Gospel, "My Kingdom is not of this world." He is a being outside the organisation created by men, outside the artificial world the adult has superimposed on nature. In the world into which he is born the child is an extra-social being *par excellence*. We call a man extra-social who cannot adapt himself to society, who cannot take an active part in its productive labours nor in the rules of its organisation, and who is thus a disturber of the established order. The fact is that the child is an extra-social being who is perpetually disturbing the adult, even in the house of his parents. His incapacity for adaptation is aggravated by the fact that he is active and cannot renounce his activity. Hence a need to make war on him; he must be taught not to interfere, not to disturb, till he is reduced to passivity. He must be relegated to living in a place apart, which, if it is not the prison assigned to extra-social adults, is something corresponding, be its name nursery, play-room or school. Here are places to which the child is banished till he can live in the adult world without disturbing it. Then he may be admitted to society. But at first he is subject to the adult like a person with no civil rights, or indeed without even civil existence, a thing of naught. The adult is his master; the child must remain at his orders, from which there is no appeal, and which are therefore considered as *a priori* just. The little child comes into the family out of nothingness, and the grown-up to him is big and powerful as a god, who alone can give him what is necessary for his life. The adult is his creator, his providence, his master, the dispenser of punishments, no one can be so utterly and wholly dependent on another as the child is on the adult.

## THE CHILD'S TASK

But the child too is a worker and a producer. If he cannot take part in the adult's work, he has his own, a great, important, difficult work indeed—the work of producing man. If from the new-born baby, helpless, unconscious, dumb, unable to raise itself, comes forth the individual adult with perfected form, with a mind enriched with all the acquisitions of his psychic life, radiant with the light of the spirit, this is the child's doing. It is the child who builds up the man, the child alone. The adult cannot take his place in this work; the exclusion of the adult from the child's "world" and "work" is still more evident and more absolute than the exclusion of the child from the work producing the social order superimposed on nature in which the adult reigns. The child's work belongs to another order and has a wholly different force from the work of the adult. Indeed one might say that the one is opposed to the other. The child's work is done unconsciously, in abandonment to a mysterious spiritual energy, actively engaged in creation. It is indeed a creative work; it is perhaps the very spectacle of the creation of man, as symbolically outlined in the Bible. A divine spirit breathed into man, of whom the scriptures say only that he was "created." But as to how he was created, how that living creature received the attributes of intelligence and power over all created things, though he himself had come from nothing, we may see and admire in all its details in the child, in every child. This wonderful spectacle is under our eyes every day. What was done was done so that it should reproduce itself in every human creature as it comes to life. There we find the living source of immortality, in which everything as it dies is renewed. We may repeat at every moment before the clear evidence of reality that the child is father to the man. All the powers of the adult come from the possibility possessed by his "child-father" to attain the full realisation of the secret pattern that was his. What, however, puts the child in the position of a real worker is that he does not fulfil the pattern of the man-to-be-made only through meditation and rest. No, his work is made up of activity, he creates by continual exercise. And we must clearly understand that he too uses his outer environment for his work, the same environment that the adult uses and transforms. It is through exercise that the child grows; his constructive activity is a real work which flows materially from his outer environment. The child in his experiences exercises himself and moves; he thus learns to co-ordinate his movements and absorbs from the outer world the emotions that give concreteness to his intelligence. He is laboriously acquiring the language, through miraculous acts of attention and through initial efforts possible to him alone. He strives irrepressibly to stand on his feet. He runs, he seeks. And in so doing he is following a programme and a time-table like the most diligent scholar in the world, with the unshakable constancy of the stars in their invisible courses. Every year it will be possible to measure his stature and he will have reached the limit assigned to him. We know that the child of five will have reached a certain level of intelligence and the child of eight another. Seeing him when he is ten, we can say how tall he is and what he can do; for the child will not disobey the programme drawn up for him by nature. Thus, through indefatigable activity, made up of efforts, experiences, conquests and grief, through harsh trials and wearisome struggles, he, step by step, fulfils his difficult and glorious task, adding always new forms of perfection. The adult indeed perfects the environment, but the child perfects being itself. His efforts are like those of a man walking without rest till he has reached his goal. Thus the perfection of the adult man depends on the child.

We, as adults, are *dependent* on him. We are the sons and dependents of the child in the sphere of his work, as he is our son and dependent in the sphere of our work. One is dependent in one sphere, the other in another. The adult is master in one sphere, but the child is master in his own sphere. And thus the one depends on the other; they are both kings, but each with his own kingdom.

This is the fundamental framework for harmony among mankind.

## THE TWO TASKS COMPARED

Since the child's work is made up of actions performed on real objects in the outer world, it may become the subject of positive study in order to ascertain its laws, its origin and the ways in which it proceeds, and to compare it with the adult's work. Both adult and child exercise an immediate action on their environments, an action that is conscious and willed, and may therefore properly be considered as work. But besides this they each have an *end* to be achieved, which is not directly known and willed. There is no vital existence, not even among the plants, that does not imply life at the expense of environment. More than that, life is an energy in the outer world, continually recomposing an environment that would otherwise disintegrate and thus constantly renewing it, holding creation in being. For example, the immediate work of the coral insects is to absorb carbonate of chalk from the sea water and to make of it a protective covering, whereas their end in respect of their environment is to create new continents. And since this end is remote from their immediate work, we may explore all there is to explore in the coral reef by scientific research, but we shall not find a new continent. The same more or less holds good for all living beings and especially for man.

Every infant being that is engaged in creating an adult being has a non-proximate end that is none the less visible and certain. Studying the child, or infant life in general, from every side, we may come to know and discover everything about it, from the atoms of its material existence to the smallest details of all its functions, but one thing we shall not find—the adult-to-be.

Now the two ends of remote and immediate action both imply work that utilises the environment.

Sometimes nature in her more simple creatures presents examples that give glimpses into some of her secrets. Among insects, for instance, we may note two forms of genuine productive work. The one is silk, the shining thread of which men spin their most precious stuffs; the other is the spider's web, the frail thread men hasten to destroy. Now silk is the work of an infant creature, the spider's web that of an adult. Indubitably we have to do with two different workers. When, therefore, we speak of the child's work and compare it with that of the adult, we speak of two different kinds of activity with different ends, but both equally real.

Now what we need to know is the character of the child's work. When a little child works he does not do so to attain an outward end. The aim of his work is the working, and when in his repetition of an exercise he brings it to an end, this end is independent of external factors. In respect of individual characteristics, the end of the work is not even an effect of weariness, for it is characteristic of the child to come forth from his labour with new vigour and full of energy. Let us say, then, that his work is the satisfaction of an inner need, a phenomenon of psychic maturation. The outer aim considered as a whole—that is, the object on which he exercises his activity, the use of that object and the end he has in view—reduces itself to a single means of inner activity. This activity is not bound up with the object as though this were a mechanical reagent determining a mechanical activity, but the mind must play its part. The repetition of the act springs from a knowledge accurately acquired both through execution and through the aims to be achieved. And all this constitutes the necessary complex motive for a formative exercise. The child feels the need to repeat this exercise not in order to perfect his performance but in order to build up his own inner being, and the time taken, the number of repetitions required, the hidden law inherent in the spiritual embryo is one of the child's secrets.

This shows one of the differences between the natural laws of adult work and those of the child's work. The child does not follow the law of the least effort, but a law directly contrary. He uses an immense amount of energy over an unsubstantial end, and he spends, not only driving energy, but intensive energy in the exact execution of every detail. The outward action and the object are therefore a means of ever transitory importance. Such a relationship between the resources of the environment and the perfecting of inner life is particularly striking, since according to the adult this very idea must inform spiritual life. The man who finds himself on a sublimated plane is not attached to outward things, but merely uses them for the moment for perfecting his inner self. Whereas the man on an ordinary plane, that is, on his own plane, is to attached to things, to outward ends, that he is ready to sacrifice himself to them and to lose his soul and his health for their sake.

Another differential feature, clear and indisputable, between the adult's work and the child's work is that the child's work permits of no exploitation of others, and no abbreviation. He must carry out the work for his development alone and he must carry it out in its entirety. No one can take over his task and grow for him. To become a man of twenty he must take twenty years. It is indeed precisely the characteristic of growing childhood to follow an inner programme and time-table unerringly, and unsparingly. Nature is a severe task-mistress who punishes the smallest disobedience by what we call arrested development, or functional deviation; in short, by illness or abnormality. It is interesting for us to pause a moment to consider the child as nature's scholar, obeying perfectly a natural energy which guides him and sets him a task which he will carry out with even more loyalty than that demanded of knights of the Middle Ages by their knightly honour. The child will grow in stature and psychological capacity, as the programme laid down by nature has ordained. As to how he does so, how he sets about his inner building, that is a secret he will not reveal—like the diligent scholar who keeps silence on what he does. Only in special circumstances will revelations be made; we might say that the child as nature's scholar must from time to time pass examinations, that is, make exceptional efforts which will lead him to achieve the various stages of his progress. Such are the sensitive periods through which all infant creatures pass, from the insect to man.

During these periods there are sensibilities characteristic of the particular stage of growth and which later disappear, and by this word sensibility we imply also a special active capacity—a power of acting which is likewise transient and characteristic of a particular stage, and which therefore must seem miraculous to those who no longer possess it. Indeed we may say that every acquisition made by a being in evolution is rendered possible by a sensitive period, just as the scholar passes examinations not only in every subject but in order to go from one grade to another in the same subject.

### GROWTH THROUGH ACTIVITY

The sensitive periods of creatures in process of evolution are one of the greatest wonders of nature. There are instincts found only during the periods of infancy, and represent an inner guidance leading to the attainment of specific characteristics. Growth is thus not something vague like a progressive accumulation of material or an inherent hereditary necessity. It is a process meticulously guided by transient instincts which give an acute sensibility and an impulse towards specific forms of activity, and these often differ very plainly from the activities of the individual in the adult state. We may say indeed that the profound difference between the two states lies in this: in reaching his full stature and his full physical development, the adult has at the same time actualised the instincts of his species, which will lead him to act in a stable manner on the outer world. Whereas the infant creature more often than not lacks the final instincts of his kind, and has instead a quantity of variable and successive instincts which will lead him to acquire the characteristics of the adult state.

Such sensibilities, the effect of the transient guiding instincts of growth, enable us to understand the incessant activity of nature. In the same way as penetrating more deeply below the outer aspect of the body we find organs and tissues functioning within, which provide a detailed explanation of the existence of a living body, with phenomena of a psychological order we may explore beneath the surface and find the different activities on which growth depends. The sensitive periods in the child sometimes endow him with truly amazing powers. We may note for instance the extraordinary keenness of a child's senses, the keenness of his eye to colours and dimensions, which guide his attention to garner the smallest details of his environment. Wonderful too is the sensitive period of order in respect of external objects and their place in the environment. It is through this sensibility that the child is able to orient himself, which would be impossible had not nature implanted such an aptitude in the infant being.

The child has a different motive principle from the adult. The adult acts in a whirl of external motives which demand great effort, sacrifice and wearisome labour. And if the adult is to be equal to his task, the child as he was must have worked well, to make of him a strong man.

He has lost his early sensibility, and nature will now find him a poor pupil who deserves to fail in her rigorous examinations. He cannot imitate the child.

The child is driven forward by delicate sensibilities aglow with intellectual love, which urge him indefatigably towards the outer world and make him garner impressions of things as a spiritual milk on which he must feed to nourish his inner life. That is why the child's psychic manifestations are at once impulses of enthusiasm and efforts of meticulous, constant patience.

The child does not grow weary with work, but increases his strength. He grows through work and that is why work increases his energies. He never asks to be relieved of his labours, but on the contrary he asks to be allowed to perform them and to perform them alone. The task of growth is his life, he must truly either work or die.

The adult who is unaware of this secret cannot understand the child's work. And, in fact, he has never understood it. That is why he has always prevented the child from working, supposing that what the child most needed in order to grow was rest. The adult has done everything *for* the child, for he has been guided only by his own natural laws of labour, the least effort and the saving of time. Quicker and more skilful than the child, the adult has dressed and undressed him, washed him, fed him, carried him about in his arms or in a perambulator, and arranged his environment without allowing the child to help.

When the child has been allowed a little room "in the world and in time," he proclaims as the first sign of his eager defence, "Me! Me want to do it!"

In the special environment prepared for them in our school, the children themselves found a sentence that expressed this inner need. "Help me to do it by myself!" How eloquent is this paradoxical request! The adult must help the child, but help him in such a way that he may act for himself and perform his real work in the world. This sentence describes not only the child's need but what he requires from his environment: he must be surrounded by a living environment, not a dead one. He wants not an environment to be mastered and enjoyed, but an environment that will help him to establish his functions. Plainly, the environment must be enlivened by a higher intelligence, arranged by an adult who is prepared for his mission. It is in this that our conception differs both from that of the world in which the adult does everything for the child and from that of a passive environment in which the adult abandons the child to himself.

The spiritual embryo, like the physical embryo, needs a living environment in which to develop.

This means that it is not enough to set the child among objects in proportion to his size and strength; the adult who is to help him must have learned how to do so. If the adult, through a fatal misunderstanding, instead of helping the child to do things for himself, substitutes himself for the child, then that adult becomes the blindest and most powerful obstacle to the development of the child's psychic life. In this misunderstanding, in the excessive competition between adult work and child work, lies the first great drama of the struggle between man and his work, and perhaps the origin of all the dramas and struggles of mankind.

Such factors at once so delicate and so far-reaching remind us of the tissues of the physical embryo, which must be sheltered, enclosed in a protective environment, so that the pattern of the form they contain shall not be spoiled. There is no doubt that for the child, the spiritual embryo of man, we must construct a protective and living environment. Now it will not be enough to put within the child's reach certain means of activity of proportionate size and destined for his use for the exercise of his constructive energies. Nor will it be enough to give a few counsels to mothers or to the adults in general who are fondest of the child and closest to him. What is needed is something on a far vaster scale. For the child shows not only desires to be satisfied but a whole life to be evolved, of which the adult has remained unconscious, and which needs most delicate care. It is no exaggeration to say that man who up till now has built only a *world for the adult* must set to work to build up a *world for the child.* The treatment of the child is so complex and so delicate that it needs something more than an awakening in the mother, or the training of new types of nurses and teachers.

The response to the child's needs must be a mental and spiritual renewal of education, which will be the centre of many collateral sciences, till the crowning result is achieved, a new outlook on life, a renewal of life.

## GUIDING INSTINCTS

In nature too, we find two forms of life, adult life and infant life, different and even contrary. Adult life is characterised by struggle, the struggle of adaptation to the environment as described by Lamarck, or the struggle of competition and natural selection described by Darwin—a struggle not only for the survival of the species but also for selection in sexual competition.

What happens among fully grown animals might be compared with the happenings in the social life of men. Here too, we find the effort of self-preservation and defence against enemies; here, too, struggles and labours to achieve adaptation to the environment, and here, too, love and sexual conquest. In such struggle and competition Darwin saw the workings of evolution, and the explanation of the survival of physical forms, just as materialistic historians have attributed the historical evolution of mankind to struggle and competition among men.

But whereas in explaining human history we have no other data than the doings of the adult, it is not so in nature. On the contrary, the real key to the life that persists and establishes itself in nature, revealing the innumerable and marvellous variety of creatures, lies in the chapter set apart for infancy. All creatures are weak before they grow strong enough to struggle, and all being at a stage where there can be no question of adaptation of their organs, for these organs do not yet exist. No living creature begins as an adult.

There is thus a hidden part of life with other forms, other resources, other motive impulses, than those apparent in the interplay between the strong individual and his environment. This chapter, the chapter of *childhood in nature,* holds the real key to life, for what happens to the adult can explain only the hazards of survival.

Biological investigations of the infant life of creatures have thrown light on the most marvellous and complex aspect of nature, revealing staggering realities, sublime possibilities, which fill all living nature with poetry and almost with religion. In this field biology has followed and brought to light the creative and conservative aspects of the species showing the existence of instincts that act as inner guides to living creatures, and which, to distinguish them from the mass of impulsive instincts connected with immediate reactions between a creature and its environment, may be termed "guiding instincts."

In biology all existing instincts have always been grouped into two fundamental classes, according to their ends, viz. instincts for the preservation of the individual and instincts for the preservation of the species. Both cases offer aspects of struggle, connected with transient episodes, and as it were, with encounters between die individual and its environment; and at the same time in both cases there are instincts that show themselves as constant vital guides, with an eminently conservative function. For instance, among the instincts for the preservation of the individual, the aspect of episodic struggle is represented by the instinct of defence against unfavourable or threatening causes. Among the instincts for the preservation of the species there is the episodic instinct aroused by encounters with other creatures in the form either of sexual union or sexual conflict. These episodic details, as the more noticeable and violent, were the first to be recognised and studied by biologists. But later on more study was devoted to the instincts for the preservation of the individual and the species in their conservative and constant aspect. These are the guiding instincts, with which is bound up the very existence of life in its great cosmic, function. Such instincts are not so much reactions to the environment as delicate inner sensibilities, *intrinsic to life,* just as pure thought is an entirely intrinsic quality of the mind. We might continue the comparison and look on them as divine thoughts working in the inmost centres of living creatures, leading them subsequently to action on the outer world in realisation of the divine plan. The guiding instincts therefore have not the impulsive character of episodic struggles, but those of an intelligence, a wisdom leading creatures on their journey through time (the individuals), and through eternity (the species).

The guiding instincts are especially wonderful when they are directed to guiding and protecting infant life at its beginnings, when a creature is still hardly in existence or immature, but is none the less on the road towards full development. At such a stage it has not acquired its racial characteristics, it has neither strength nor resistance nor the biological weapons of struggle, nor hope of a final victory as the sure prize of survival. Here the guiding instinct acts as at once a form of maternity and a form of education, and both are mysterious like the secret of creation. Such guidance carries a helpless creature to safety when it has in itself neither material nor strength to save itself.

One of these guiding instincts concerns motherhood, the wonderful instinct described by Fabre and by modem biologists as the key to the survival of creatures. The other concerns the development of the individual, and has been dealt with by the Dutch biologist, De Vries, in his study of the sensitive periods.

The maternal instinct is not confined to the mother, though she, as direct procreatrix of the species, has the largest share in this task of protection. It is to be found in both parents, and sometimes pervades a whole social group of creatures. A profounder study of what is known as the maternal instinct leads us to recognize it as a mysterious energy, which is not necessarily associated with living creatures, but which exists as a protection to the species even without maternal vehicle, as in the words of the *Book of Ecclesiasticus,* "From the beginning, and before the world, was I created."

The term maternal instinct is thus a generic term for the guiding instinct of preservation of the species. There are certain characteristics which dominate this domain in all species; the maternal instinct means a sacrifice of all other instincts existing in the adult for ensuring its survival. The fiercest animal will show a gentleness and tenderness at variance with its nature; the bird which flies so far in search of food or to flee from danger, will remain still to watch over its nest, finding other means of defending itself from danger, but never that of flight. Instincts inherent in the species suddenly change in character. Besides this, in many species, a tendency to construction and work appears such as is never found in the same creatures at other times, for once arrived at the adult state they adapt themselves to nature as they find it. The new instinct of protection of the species leads to a constructive labour so as to prepare a dwelling and shelter for the new-born young.... In this every species and variety of creatures obey a special guidance. None takes the first material it finds within its reach, or adapts its manner of building to locality. No, its instructions are definite and unvarying. The manner of building the nest, for instance, is one of the differential characteristics of the different varieties of birds. Among insects we find stupendous examples of constructive work; the hives of bees are palaces of a perfectly geometrical architecture, which a whole society has combined to build to house the new generation. There are other less striking cases which are none the less extremely interesting, like spiders, which are exceptional in that they build also for themselves, and know how to stretch such wide and slender nets for their enemies. All at once the spider radically changes her work and, forgetting her own necessities, begins to make a tiny sack of new, very fine, densely woven tissues, which are quite waterproof. Often the sack has double walls, making it an excellent shelter in the damp, cold places in which certain varieties of spiders live. There is thus real wisdom in regard to the exigencies of the climate. Inside, in safety, the spider lays her eggs. But what is strange is that she has a passionate attachment to her sack. In certain laboratory observations it has been noticed that such spiders, with their grey, slimy bodies in which no amount of searching will ever find a heart, can die of grief if their sack is torn and destroyed. In fact, it has been discovered that the spider, where she can, remains as attached to her work as if the sack were an extension of her body. She loves the sack, but she has no feeling for the eggs, nor for the tiny live spiders that will come forth from them. She seems indeed quite unaware of their existence. Instinct has led this mother to work for the species without having the living creature of the species as direct object. There can thus be an *instinct without direct object,* acting irresistibly, representing an obedience to an inner command to do what is necessary, and bringing a love for what has been commanded.

There are butterflies which, their whole lives through, suck the nectar of flowers without being aware of any other enticements or any other food. But when the time comes for them to lay their eggs, they never lay them on flowers. They are then otherwise guided; the food-seeking instinct proper to the individual changes, and they are led to seek another environment, one that is suited to a new species needing other food. And yet these butterflies are unaware of such food, just as they will never know the species that is to come. They bear in themselves a command of nature, foreign to their own being. The cochineal insect and others similar never lay their eggs on the upper side of the leaves that will serve as food to the tiny grubs, but on their under surfaces, so that the grubs may be sheltered and hidden. We find like "intelligent reflection" among a large number of insects, which also never eat the plants they choose for their offspring. They have therefore a "theoretical" knowledge of how their young will feed, and they even "foresee" the dangers of rain and sun.

The adult creature with the mission of protecting the new creatures, thus changes its characteristics and transforms its own nature, as though a time had come in which the usual law governing its life stood still in expectation of a great event in nature—the miracle of creation. Then it does something that is not just living but, one might say, carries out a rite to be performed in the presence of this miracle.

One of nature's most resplendent miracles is indeed the power of the newly born, with no experience at all, to find their way about and protect themselves in the outer world, guided by partial and transitory instincts which show themselves as *Sensitive Periods*. Here the instinct is truly and literally a guide leading them gradually through successive difficulties and animating the new creatures with irresistible power. It is plain that nature has not surrendered the protection of the newly born to the adult; she holds the reins tight and keeps a vigilant watch on the observance of her precepts. The adult must collaborate within the limits set by the guiding instincts for the protection of the species. Often, as we see in fishes and insects, the two forms of guiding instinct, that in the adult and that in the new creature, act separately and independently, when parents and children never meet. In higher animals, on the other hand, the two instincts gradually converge in the meeting of parent and offspring, and harmonious collaboration ensues. It is in the encounter of the maternal guiding instincts with the sensitive periods of the newly born that conscious love develops between parent and child. Or else maternal relations may extend to the whole of an organised society, which treats the new offspring as a whole, the living products of a race. This we find among social insects like bees, ants, and so forth.

Love and sacrifice are not the cause of the protection of the species, but the effects of an animating guiding instinct of which the roots stretch down to the grandiose creative laboratory of life, from which every species draws its forces of survival. Affectionate feeling only renders the task imposed an easier one, giving to effort that especial delight that is found in perfect obedience to the order of nature.

If we wished to embrace the whole adult world in a single glance, we might say that from time to time there is a breach of the laws proper to it, the laws that are most apparent in nature and which therefore are believed to be absolute and unchangeable. And lo! these invincible laws are broken: they stay their working, as though to leave place for something higher, and they bow before factors in contradiction to themselves. That is to say, they remain suspended to further new laws which appear in the infant life of the species. It is thus that life is maintained; it is renewed by such suspension, which allows it to reach inward towards eternity.

Now we may ask, what is the part of man in these laws of nature? Man, it is said, contains in himself as in a supreme synthesis all the natural phenomena of the beings beneath him; he epitomises and transcends them. And what is more, by the privilege of mind, he enhances them with the sparkling splendour of that psychic vestment which is made up of imagination, feeling and art.

How then are the two forms of life presented in mankind and under what sublime aspects do they reveal themselves? The fact is, the two lives are not apparent. Seek as we will through the world of men, we must say that it embraces only a world of adults of which the prevailing features are struggle, efforts at adaptation, and labour for outward conquests. The events of the world of men all converge on conquest and production, as though there were nothing else to be considered. Human effort clashes and is broken in competition, like a tempered blade against a breastplate. If the adult considers the child, he does so with the logic he brings to bear on his own life. He sees in the child a different and useless creature and he keeps him at a distance; or else through what is called education, he endeavours to draw him prematurely and directly into the forms of his own life. He acts as one might imagine a butterfly acting were it to break the chrysalis of its larva to bid it fly or a frog were it to drag its tadpoles out of the water, doing its best to make them breathe through lungs and change their ugly black colour for green.

That is more or less what man does to his children. The adult exhibits before them his own perfection, his own maturity, his own historical example, calling upon the child to imitate him. He is far from realising that the different characteristics of the child need a different environment and means of life suited to this other form of existence.

How can we explain such a mistaken conception in the loftiest, furthest evolved being, gifted with a mind of his own? who is the dominator of his environment, the creature full of power, able to work with an immeasurable superiority over all other living things?

Yet he, the architect, the builder, the producer, the transformer of his environment, does less for his child than the bees, than the insects, and any other creature.

Can the highest and most essential guiding instinct of life be totally absent in mankind? Can mankind be truly helpless and blind before the most staggering phenomenon of universal life, upon which the existence of the species depends?

Man should feel something of what other creatures feel, for in nature everything is transformed but nothing is lost, and the energies that govern the universe are especially indestructible. They persist even when deviated from their proper object.

Where does man, the builder, build especially for his child? The child should live in an environment of beauty, in which man expresses his loftiest forms of art, an art that is not contaminated or determined by any outward need, in which an impulse of generous love stores up riches that cannot be utilised in the world of production. Are there places where man feels the need to suspend and forget his usual characteristics, where he perceives that the essential thing that maintains life is something other than struggle? Where he perceives as a truth rising from the deep that to oppress others is not the secret of survival or the important thing in life, but of purely individual concern? Where therefore a surrender of self seems truly life-giving? Is there no place where the soul aspires to break though the iron laws that hold it bound to the world of outward things? Is there no anxious quest for a miracle, a need for a miracle to continue life? And at the same time an aspiration towards something beyond the furthest span of individual life, stretching into eternity? It is on this road that salvation lies. In such places man feels the need to renounce his laborious reasoning and is ready to believe. For all these are the feelings that should be aroused in man by facts analogous to those that lead all living creatures to a suspension of the laws of their nature, to a holocaust of themselves, so that life may be carried forward towards eternity. Yes, there are places where man no longer feels the need for conquest, but the need for purification and innocence, so that he yearns for simplicity and peace. In that innocent peace, man seeks a renewal of life, as it was a resurrection from the weight of the world.

Yes, there must be grandiose feelings in man, diverse from those of everyday life and opposed to them.

This is the divine voice that no one can still, and which calls men with a loud voice, calling them together to gather round the child.

# 11

## The Child as Master

### "KNOW THYSELF"

To trace the guiding instincts in man is one of the most important subjects of research for the present day. We ourselves have started such investigation and we have brought it from non-existence to a beginning. In this our chief contribution to the question lies. It opens the new road of investigation and its results till now have been a proof of the existence of such instincts and a first outline of how they should be studied.

Their study is only possible in the normalised child, who lives in freedom in an environment fitted to the needs of his development. Then a new nature shows itself, with such clarity that its normal characters impose themselves as indisputable realities.

Innumerable experiences have shown us a truth that equally concerns two domains, that of education and that of the social organisation of mankind. It is plain that the social organisation of men of different nature from that commonly known, should itself be different, and it is education that may point the way to a normalisation of the adult world also. Such a social reform would not come about through theory or the energies of a few organisers, but through the slow constant emergence of a new world in the midst of the old—the world of the child and of the adolescent. From this world the revelations, the natural guidance necessary to the normal life of society, would gradually evolve. It is truly absurd to suppose that theoretical reforms or individual energies could remedy so colossal a void as that made in the world by the repression of the child. No one can remedy the ever-growing evils of which the first roots lie in the fact that men are all *abnormal* because their infancy could not develop along the lines traced by nature, who therefore suffered irremediable deviation.

The unknown energy that can help humanity is that which lies hidden in the child.

To-day it is time to revive the dictum: "Know thyself." It is the source of all the biological sciences which have helped to better and save the physical life of man through modern medicine and hygiene, marking what is almost the level of a higher civilisation, a civilisation characterised by physical hygiene.

But in the domain of the mind man is still unknown to himself. The first researches when he sought to know his physical self were carried out on the bodies of the dead. The first researches to know his psychic self deal with the *living* man as soon as he is born.

Without these basic considerations it would seem that there is no way open to progress or indeed, one might almost say, to the survival of humanity in our civilisation. All the problems involved in social questions must remain unsolved, like the problems envisaged in modern scientific pedagogy. For an improvement in education can have only one basis, the normalization of the child. Once this is obtained, not only do pedagogic problems become soluble, but indeed they no longer present themselves. And, what is more, the results obtained are as unlocked for and amazing as miracles.

Maybe the same procedure is required for adult humanity and here there is only one true problem, that implied by the words "Know thyself"— knowledge of the underlying laws that guide the psychic development of man. But the child has already solved this problem, and a practical path has been opened. Outside this, there is no sign of any salvation practically possible. For every good thing comes down upon deviated men who seek to possess it for themselves, and seek to make of it a means to power. Then the good thing is destroyed even before it can be of service, and thus becomes a danger to human life. That is why every good thing, all progress, all discoveries, can increase the evil afflicting the world, as we have seen in the case of machines, which represent the most tangible form of social progress for us all. Every discovery that might mean elevation and progress can be used for destruction, for war, or for self-enrichment. The progress of physics, chemistry and biology, the perfecting of means of transport, have only magnified the danger of destruction, wretchedness and the appearance of a cruel barbarity. We have therefore nothing to hope from the external world till the normalisation of man is recognised as a basic achievement of social life. Only then will all external progress be able to lead to welfare and a higher civilisation.

We must therefore turn to the child as to the key to the fate of our future life. Anyone wishing to succeed in some aim for the good of society, must necessarily turn to the child, not only to save him from deviation, but also to learn from him the practical secret of our own life. From this point of view the figure of the child presents itself as powerful and mysterious, an object of meditation, for the child who holds in himself the secret of our nature becomes our master.

### THE PARENTS' MISSION

The child's parents are not his makers but his guardians. They must protect and care for him, in the deepest sense as a sacred mission that goes far beyond the interests and ideas of external life. They are for him supernatural guardians, to be compared to the guardian angels of theology, who depend directly and solely on heaven, who have a power superior to that of any human authority, and who, united to the child in a way of which he is unaware, cannot be separated from him. For such a mission parents must purify the love nature has implanted in their hearts, and they must understand that such love is the conscious part of a deeper guidance which must not be contaminated by egotism or apathy. It is for parents to visualise and take up the social question facing us at the present day, the struggle to establish the rights of the child in the world.

Much has been said of recent years about the rights of man, and especially about the rights of the worker, but now the time has come when we must speak of the social rights of the child. The social question of the rights of the worker has been the basis of social transformations, for humanity lives by the work of men, and hence this question was connected with the material existence of humanity as a whole. But if the worker produces what man consumes, and is a creator in external things, the child produces mankind itself, and therefore his rights are still more powerful in calling for social transformation. It is plain that human society should direct its wisest and most perfect care to the child, to receive from him greater strength and greater values in the humanity of the future.

The fact that it has instead neglected and indeed forgotten the rights of the child, that it has, maybe unconsciously, tormented and broken him down, has failed to recognise his value, his power, his essential nature, should be realised and this feeling should arouse the conscience of humanity in a most vehement manner.

## THE RIGHTS OF THE CHILD

Till yesterday, till the beginning of the present century, society showed not the smallest concern for the child. It left him where he was born, to the sole care of his family. As his sole protection and defence, there was the authority of the father, which is more or less a relic of that established by Roman law over two thousand years ago. During so long a period of time, civilisation evolved, changing its laws in favour and in the service of the adult, but it left the child without any social defence. To him were reserved only the material, moral or intellectual resources of the family into which he was born. And if in his family there were no such resources, the child had to develop in material, moral and intellectual misery, without society's feeling the smallest responsibility for him. Society up till now has never claimed that the family should prepare itself in any way to receive and fittingly care for the children that might come to form part of it. The State, so rigorous in demanding official documents and meticulous preparations, and which so loves to regulate everything that bears the smallest trace of social responsibility, does not trouble to ascertain the capacity of future parents to give adequate protection to their children or to guard their development. It has provided no place of instruction or preparation for parents. As far as the State is concerned, it is enough for anyone wishing to found a family to go through the marriage ceremony. In view of all this, we may well declare that society from the earliest times has washed its hands of those little workers to whom nature has entrusted the task of building up humanity. In the midst of a continual progress in favour of the adult they have remained as beings not belonging to human society, extra-social, isolated, without any means of communication that would allow society to become aware of their condition. They might be victims without society's being aware.

And, in truth, they were victims.

Victims indeed, as science recognised, when about half a century ago medicine began to interest itself in childhood. At that time childhood was still more abandoned than to-day, there were neither child specialists nor children's hospitals. Only when statistics revealed so high a mortality during the first year of life was a sensation caused. People began to reflect that though many children were born into families, few remained alive. The death of small children seemed so natural that families had accustomed themselves to it, comforting themselves with thought that such little children went straight to heaven. There had come to be a special spiritual preparation teaching resigned submission to this kind of recruitment of little angels, whom, it was said, God wished to have near Him. Such vast numbers of babies died through ignorance or lack of proper care that the phenomenon was termed the constant "slaughter of innocents."

The facts were made public and at once an extensive propaganda was organised to awaken social conscience to a new sense of responsibility. It was not enough for families to give life to their children, but they must save that life. And science showed how this could be done: fathers and mothers must gain new knowledge and receive the instruction necessary for a proper care of the health of their babies.

But it was not only in families that children suffered. Scientific investigations in the schools led to alarming revelations of torment. And this was in the last decade of the 19th century—at a time when medicine was discovering and studying industrial diseases among workers, and showing the first steps to be taken for social hygiene in work. It was then acknowledged that besides infectious diseases resulting from unhygienic conditions children too had their "industrial" diseases—caused by their work.

Their work lay in the schools. They were shut up there, exposed to the enforced torments of society. The narrow chest that brought an acquired predisposition to tuberculosis, came from long hours spent bending over desks, learning to read and write. The spinal column was curved through the same enforced position; eyes were short-sighted through the prolonged effort of trying to see without sufficient light. The whole body was deformed and as it were asphyxiated, through long periods spent in small, overcrowded spaces.

Yet their torment was not only physical; it extended to mental work. Studies were forced studies, and what with tedium and fear, the children's minds were tired, their nervous systems exhausted. They were lazy, prejudiced, discouraged, melancholic, vicious, with no faith in themselves, with none of the lovely gaiety of childhood.

Unhappy children! Oppressed children!

Their families realised nothing of all this. What concerned them was that their children should pass their examinations and learn their lessons as quickly as possible, so as to save time and money. It was not learning in itself, the attainment of a loftier culture that concerned the families, but the response to the summons of society, to the obligation imposed, an obligation which they found burdensome and which cost money. What was therefore important was that their sons should acquire their passport into the life of society in the shortest time possible.

Enquiries and investigations then carried out among school-children brought to light other startling facts. Many poor children, when they came to school, were already tired out by their morning's labours. Before going to school some of them had walked miles to distribute milk, or had gone running and shouting though the streets, selling newspapers, or had been working at home. They reached school hungry, sleepy, with the sole wish to rest. These poor little victims then received a larger share of punishments, for they could not pay attention to their teacher and so did not understand his explanations. And the teacher, concerned for his responsibility and still more for his authority, tried by punishment to awaken the interest of these worn out children and to drive them to obedience by threats. He would humiliate them before all their school-fellows, for incapacity or obstinacy. Such unfortunate children spent their lives exploited at home and punished at school.

The injustice revealed by these first investigations and enquiries was such that it led to a genuine social reaction. The schools and the relevant regulations were speedily modified. A new and important branch of medicine was inaugurated, covering school health and exercising a protective and regenerating influence on all the recognized schools of civilised countries. Doctor and teacher were henceforth associated for the good of the pupils. This was, we may say, the first social sanction against an ancient unconscious error in the whole of humanity and it marked the first step towards the social redemption of the child.

If we look back from this initial awakening and follow the course of history, we shall find no salient fact revealing a recognition of the rights of the child, or an intuitive awareness of his importance. Christ alone called them to Him pointing them out to adult man as his guides to the Kingdom of Heaven, and warning him of his blindness. He warned us: "Unless you convert and become like little children, you will never enter the Kingdom of Heaven." But the adult continued to think only of converting the child, putting himself before him as an example of perfection. It seemed as if this terrible blindness was incurable. Mystery of the human soul! This blindness has remained a universal phenomenon and is perhaps as old as mankind.

In fact in every educational ideal, in all pedagogy up to our own time, the word education has been almost always synonymous with the word punishment. The end was always to subject the child to the adult, who substituted himself for nature, and set his reasoning and his will in the place of the laws of life. Different nations have different ways of punishing children. In private schools the punishments in use are often pointed out as they might point out their coat of arms. Some use humiliations, like tying placards to the children's backs, putting dunces' caps on their heads or putting them in a real pillory so that those who pass can laugh at them and mock them. Often the punishments used are physical tortures. Children are put to stand in a corner for several hours, tired, bored by idleness, seeing nothing, but condemned to hold their position by their own will.

Other punishments are to make them kneel on the floor with bare knees, or whipping, or public caning. A modern refinement of cruelty comes from the theory of associating school and family in the work of education—a principle which resolves itself into organising school and family in inflicting punishment and tormenting the child. The child who is punished in school must consign his sentence to his father, so that the father may join with the teacher in punishing him and scolding him.

He is then forced to take back to school a writing from his father, as a proof that he has accused himself to his other executioner, who associated himself, at least in principle, with the persecution of his own son. Thus the child is condemned to carry his own cross.

There is no one to defend him. Where is the tribunal to whom the child can appeal, as condemned criminals appeal? It does not exist. Where is the love in which the child knows that he will find refuge and consolation? It is not there. School and family are agreed in punishing him, for if this were not so the punishment would be lessened and thus education would be abased.

But the family does not need reminders from school to punish its children. Investigations recently carried out on the punishments in use in families (and one such enquiry was carried out on the initiative of the League of Nations) show that even in our own time there is no country great or small in the world where children are not punished in their families. They are violently scolded, abused, beaten, slapped, kicked, driven out of sight, shut up in dark, frightening rooms, threatened with fantastic perils, or deprived of the little reliefs which are their refuge in their perpetual slavery or the solace of torments unconsciously endured, such as playing with their friends or eating sweets or fruit. And finally there is the familiar punishment of fasting inflicted usually in the evening, to go to bed without supper, so that, all night through, sleep is disturbed by grief and hunger.

Although among educated families punishments have rapidly diminished, they are still in use, and rough manners, a harsh, severe and threatening voice, are usual forms of behaviour towards a child. It seems natural that the adults should have the right to chastise the child, that his mother should feel it her duty to slap him.

And yet arbitrary and public corporal punishment has been abolished for the adult, because it lowers his dignity and is a social disgrace. And yet what greater baseness can be conceived than that of insulting and beating a child? It is evident that the conscience of humanity lies buried in a deep sleep.

The progress of civilisation today does not depend on individual progress, it does not spring from the burning flame of the human soul, it is the advance of an insensible machine, driven by an external force. The energy that moves it emanates from the outer world, like an immense impersonal power coming from society as a whole, and functioning inexorably. Forward! Ever forward!

Society is like a huge train travelling with a vertiginous velocity towards a distant point, while the individuals composing it are like travellers, asleep in their compartments. It is in that sleeping conscience that we find the mightiest obstacle to any vital aid or saving truth. If this were not so, the world would be able to progress rapidly; there would not be the perilous contrast between the ever greater speed of material transport and the ever deeper-reaching rigidity of the human spirit. The first step, the most difficult in any social movement towards a collective progress, is the task of awakening this sleeping and insensible humanity and of forcing it to listen to the voice that calls it.

Today it is necessary that society as a whole should become aware of the child and of his importance, and that it should rapidly remedy the peril of the vast void on which it rests. It must fill that void by building the world for the child and recognising his social rights. The greatest crime that society is committing is that of wasting the money it should spend for its children, of dissipating it to destroy them and itself. Society has acted like a guardian who dissipates the capital belonging to his ward. The adult world spends and builds for itself alone, whereas clearly a great part of its wealth should be destined for the child. This truth is inherent in life itself; the animals, the humblest insect, can teach it to us. For whom do the ants store up food? For whom do the bees suck nectar? For whom do the birds seek the food they carry to their nests? There is no example in nature of adults devouring everything themselves and leaving their offspring in want. Yet nothing is done for the human child; there is just the bare endeavour to preserve his body in a state of vegetative life. When wasteful society has urgent need of money, it takes it from the schools and especially from the infant schools that shelter the seeds of human life. It takes it from where there are neither arms nor voices to defend it. And therefore this is humanity's worst crime and most absurd error. Society does not even perceive that it destroys twice over when it uses that money for instruments of destruction; it destroys by not enabling life and it destroys by bringing death. And the two are one and the same error, for it is precisely through failing to assure the development of life that men have grown up in an abnormal manner.

Adults must now organise afresh and this time not for themselves but for their children. They must raise their voices to claim a right that they cannot see through their innate blindness, but which, once seen, is indisputable. If society has been a faithless guardian to the child, it must now make restitution of his goods and give him justice.

There is a mighty mission before all parents. They alone can and must save their children, for they have the power to organise socially, and hence to act in the practice of associated life. Their consciences must feel the force of the mission entrusted to them by nature, a mission which sets them above society, which enables them to dominate all material circumstances, for in their hands lies positively the future of humanity, life.

If they will not do so, they will act like Pontius Pilate.

Pilate in Palestine was all-powerful, for he had the might of Rome behind him, the imperial power dominating all other powers.

Pilate could have saved Jesus. He could have, but he did not.

The mob with their ancient prejudices, over-attached to the laws in force, to ancient custom, demanded the death of the innocent, the Redeemer, and Pilate remained undecided and inert.

"What can I do," he must have thought, "if these are the prevailing customs?"

And he washed his hands.

He had the power to say: "No, I will not!" But he did not say it.

Parents today behave like Pilate, they abandon their children to social custom, which is so powerful as to seem a necessity.

And thus the social tragedy of the child takes its course. Society abandons the child, without feeling the smallest responsibility, to the care of his family and the family, for its part, gives up the child to society which shuts him in school, isolating him from all family control.

Thus the child repeats the Passion of Christ driven from Herod to Pilate, tossed between the two powers, who each leave Him to the responsibility of the other.

No voice is raised in the child's defence, and yet there is a voice that should have power to defend him, the voice of blood, the power of life, the human authority of his parents.

When the consciences of parents awaken they will not act like Pilate, who to defend the Messiah denied His divinity, bound Him, scourged Him, and was the first to humiliate Him, saying "Ecce homo!"

This act history judges not as a defence of Christ, but as the first episode of his Passion.

## ECCE HOMO

Yes, the child will pass through a passion, like the Passion of Christ.

But the beginning of all lies in the *Ecce Homo*. Behold the man. There is no God in him. He is empty, and he has been humiliated and beaten by the higher authority that could defend him.

After that he is dragged away by the crowd, by social authority. For the child the school has been a place of more than natural woe. Those big buildings seem made for a host of grown-up people, and everything is proportionate to the adult—the windows, the doors, the grey corridors, the bare, blank walls. There the child of many, many generations puts on the black uniform of mourning which would last through the whole period of childhood. On the threshold his family left him, for that door was forbidden them. Here was the separation of the two domains and the two responsibilities. And to the child, weeping and without hope, his heart shaken by fear, it was as if he read on the door Dante's inscription over the gates of Hell:

"Through me men go into the city of weeping,

Through me men pass to the people of the lost."

It was a stern, threatening voice that summoned him to come in with other unknown companions, judged *en masse* as wicked creatures, who must be punished. Again Dante's verse comes to mind:

"Woe unto you, evil souls."

Where will the child go?

He will go where he is ordered, where he is sent.

He has been judged. He will go into a class room, and someone will do as Dante's Minos, who, twisting his tail round his body, showed the lost soul to which circle it was destined. But everywhere there is eternal woe, with no escape.

When the child has gone in, into the class assigned to him, a teacher will *shut the* door. Henceforth she is mistress, she commands that group of souls, with no witness or control.

She will shut the door.

Family and society have surrendered their children to her authority. Men have scattered their own seed to the wind, and thither the wind has carried it. Henceforth those delicate, trembling limbs are held to the wood for more than three hours of anguish, three and three for many days, and months and years.

The child's hands and feet are fastened to the desk by stern looks, which hold them motionless as the nails of the Cross in the body of Christ. The two little feet still and together, the two little hands joined and still, resting on the desk. And when into the mind athirst for truth and knowledge the ideas of the teacher are forcibly driven, as he wills, the little head humbled in submission will seem to bleed as by a crown of thorns.

The little heart so full of love will be pierced by the incomprehension of the world as by a lance. The culture offered to quench that thirst for knowledge will seem very bitter.

The tomb of the soul that was not able to live in a world, so artificial, with all its camouflages, is already prepared and when it is laid there, guards as though in mockery will be set round to see that it does not rise again.

But the child rises always, and returns, fresh and made anew, to live among men.

As Emerson says, the child is the eternal Messiah continually descending among fallen men, to lead them to the Kingdom of Heaven.